GOD'S OU

William Tyndale

BRIAN H. EDWARDS

GOD'S OUTLAW

EVANGELICAL PRESS

EVANGELICAL PRESS
Faverdale North Industrial Estate, Darlington, DL3 OPH, England

© Evangelical Press 1976

First published 1976
This edition 1988
Second impression 1993
Third impression 1996
Fourth impression 1998
Fifth impression 1999

British Library Cataloguing in Publication Data available

ISBN 0 85234 253 5

For current information on the
Persecuted Church contact:

The Voice of the Martyrs, Inc.
PO Box 443
Bartlesville, OK 74005
(918) 337-8015

Printed and bound in Great Britain by Creative Print and Design
Wales, Ebbw Vale.

To my parents.

Brian H. Edwards.

CONTENTS

ILLUSTRATIONS

Frontispiece: William Tyndale.

Page 47

Little Sodbury Manor, from a print dated 1750.

(Line drawing by Ken Reynolds)

Page 59

An early drawing of the Great Hall at Little Sodbury Manor as it was at the time of Tyndale's historic decision to translate the Scriptures into English.

(Reproduced by courtesy of the British Museum)

Page 64

A section of Old London Bridge showing the cellars beneath the Thames embankment in which copies of Tyndale's New Testament were hidden by the merchants.

(A line drawing by Ken Reynolds from a pen and wash drawing by Keirinck dated April 18th, 1627)

Page 86

From a painting by Alexander Johnston (1815-1891) entitled "Tyndale translating the Bible" and originally completed in 1854.

(Line drawing by Peter Wagstaff)

Page 98

A page showing the opening of the Acts of the Apostles from the only complete copy of Tyndale's 1526 New Testament known to exist.

(Reproduced by courtesy of the Bristol Baptist College, England)

ACKNOWLEDGEMENTS

Among the many public and private libraries that have helpfully assisted in the preparation of this book, the author would particularly acknowledge his debt to the late Mr Gordon Sayer, Librarian at the Evangelical Library, London, and to the staff at Surbiton Public Library, at the Gloucester Public Library, and at the Dr Williams Library, London. Special thanks are also due to the Rev. Keith Ensor, Rector of Horton and Little Sodbury, for his kind help and encouragement, and to Mrs Harford, the present occupier of Little Sodbury Manor. Appreciation must also be expressed to the Principal and Librarian of the Baptist College in Bristol for access to the 1526 edition of Tyndale's New Testament.

NOTE

Unless otherwise stated, all quotations from the New Testament are taken from Tyndale's 1526 Worms edition. Other quotations from Tyndale and his contemporaries are generally reproduced with modern spelling for ease of reading. Some passages have retained the original spelling. The difference will be obvious!

Chapter 1

BATTLE ROYAL

1513

The quiet, serious student shuffled into the lecture hall, shivered, and buried his feet in a pile of rushes. It was six o'clock in the morning and he had already attended chapel at five. The students huddled alongside one another for warmth and prepared for the dull, three hour lecture that would follow. William Tyndale looked around at the bare, cheerless room, with its large, shuttered windows and tiled floor strewn with rushes. Everything was dismal and cold, yet typical of the seven or eight colleges that made up the university town of Oxford in 1513. The lecture, without heart or life, rambled on for three boring hours until, around ten o'clock, William trooped out to the dining hall; here he shared a penny piece of beef with three friends and sat down to his bowl of broth and a lump of hard oatmeal cake. The meal finished, the students returned to their lectures until five when supper was served, not much better than their lunch.

Student life was harsh and many of the young men maintained themselves in food, lodging, clothes and amusements for fifty shillings a year. They were too poor to work by candle-light during the long winter evenings, and studies therefore continued in the form of debates and discussions; in this way a number of students could share one candle. At nine or ten o'clock, being without fire, they would run about for half an hour to generate sufficient heat before going to bed. The undergraduate was invariably in his middle teens, and the lot of the graduate was little better than that

of his junior. It was perfectly acceptable for many of the
students to beg, both in the town and on their way home for
the three months' summer vacation; it was considered an act
of charity to give to the pale and ill-clad student.

But most students could look forward to a better future.
Their frugal days of study would soon break into rich
livings in the Church, or the ample rewards of the manage-
ment of a family estate; it was a small sacrifice to bear now,
in anticipation of the luxury and ease that would follow.

William Tyndale threw himself into his studies unaware
of what lay before him. With no large family estate, and a
growing unrest with the Church within his soul, nothing
was certain. And it was as well that the young graduate
did not know the course that lay ahead. For almost all of
the remaining twenty-two years of his life, Tyndale would
own no home and receive no assured income. He was
destined to live in poverty, and as an outlaw in constant fear
for his life. Every daylight hour, and as far as his meagre
candle-money would allow, long into the night also, he would
be found hunched over his desk squinting in the half-light
at the books before him, and carefully inscribing on the bare
sheets that lay to hand words that would change the heart of
England. Unknown to the young scholar he was shortly to
enter a contest that would give to England its most price-
less treasure and rob it of its finest men; a contest that
would demand of William Tyndale the unceasing labour
of his remaining years, but would issue in the first English
New Testament in print and in the cruel death of its translator. It was to be a battle that would change the course of
history, and a battle in which every man would be involved
from pope to ploughman. Few would be more involved
than the King of England himself who, in this very year, was
sailing across the channel eager to dazzle the world with his
magnificence and ignorant of the importance of the frail
scholar at Oxford.

ALL THE KING'S MEN

At seven o'clock on the evening of Thursday 30th June, 1513
the last ships carrying a magnificent invasion army arrived

at Calais. Guns from the fleet and the town garrison roared so mightily that one observer commented the world might well be coming to an end; the thunder could be heard at Dover twenty-two miles away. This was merely the personal greeting of Sir Gilbert Talbot, the governor, to his twenty-two year old king Henry VIII. Calais had been an English possession since its capture by Edward III more than a century and a half earlier. Henry, resplendent in his armour covered with a tunic of cloth of gold embroidered with the red cross of St. George, graciously acknowledged the citizens' welcome and settled himself in for a month of entertainment before he began his war.

Two years earlier the young king had begun to flex his war muscles; not that, in reality, he had any to flex other than half a dozen ships, a small, picturesque, but ill-trained army, and an inordinate pride in the conviction that English is best. In 1512 an expeditionary force had sweltered in the Spanish sun until it ran out of beer and then, in defiance of its officers, packed up and came home. Such a thing would not happen this time. Henry would lead the invasion of France in person and the whole world would hear and see the glittering splendour of the English army.

The invading force consisted of between thirty to forty thousand men in full harness, and its magnificence, pageantry and flamboyance formed a fitting swan song to the Middle Ages. No army was ever again seen to compare with this one – and that was just about Henry's only tangible achievement. The army was divided into three sections: the fore-ward, middle-ward and rear-ward. The king was in the middle, of course, and his part of the force contained about sixteen thousand men of whom over two thousand were there just to wait upon His Majesty. The king's wardrobe staff numbered forty-nine with another fifteen to look after his beds; there were one hundred and fifteen on his chapel staff and five hundred and seventy-nine ushers, grooms, pages, and general servants. Eight trumpeters and ten minstrels and players were added and, presumably in case the king came too close to the battle, thirty-one of His

Majesty's physicians, surgeons and their assistants. On the
principle that the best soldier is well clothed, well fed and
comfortably billeted, the king's "wardrobe of beds and
wardrobe of robes" required seven hundred square feet of
marquee each.

The king was virtually impregnable. When he rode out
during the day he was encased in sixty pounds of ornamental
steel, and when he retired at night he was snugly enclosed
in a portable, prefabricated timber house with two rooms,
the larger one measuring twenty-seven feet by fourteen feet
by eight feet high, complete with fireplace and chimney. It
was painted red outside and hung with golden tapestry
inside. Twelve wagons were required to transport this
palace.

But it was not only the king who determined to fight this
war in comfort. The Earl of Northumberland carried with
him a feather bed together with "cushions of silk, hangings
of worsted, twelve dishes, six saucers, twelve silver spoons,
two or three folding stools, a folding table, a close carriage
with seven horses, two chariots each with eight horses, four
carts each with seven horses (presumably for the earl's
personal belongings), not to speak of a steward, a chamber-
lain, and a treasurer of the household, a treasurer of war,
two chaplains, a gentleman usher of the chamber, a master
of the horse, carvers, cupbearers, a herald and a pursuivant",
and Northumberland merely brought up the rear!

Thomas Wolsey, the king's Almoner who was already
clawing his way to power, lived only a little less splendidly
than the king with seventeen hundred square feet of marquee
at his disposal.

In addition to the trappings, there had to be room for
food and ammunition. Wolsey had ordered the slaughter of
twenty-five thousand oxen for the occasion, supplemented
by one thousand sheep. And with a beer allowance of almost
a gallon for each man per day and a food allowance of
ten pounds of meat and biscuit, Wolsey required a fleet of
wagons for drink and meat alone. Henry was well aware that
the bow and arrow were rapidly being made obsolete by a
new and more effective form of artillery and, accordingly,

his army dragged with it six enormous bombards, or
cannons, each weighing over two tons. Incredibly they were
capable of firing twelve-inch diameter iron balls weighing
two hundred and sixty pounds, with an eighty pound charge
of gunpowder. Apart from their weight (and it required
twenty-four Flemish mares to pull each), they had the disadvantage of a massive recoil and such overheating that
they could only be fired five times a day! But this was not all;
Henry ordered twelve cannons specially for the occasion.
Apparently six were large and six slightly smaller, but their
combined weight exceeded twenty-seven tons. Each cannon
was named after one of the twelve apostles and was capable
of firing a twenty-pound iron ball at a rate of thirty a day.
Including its equipment the heaviest of the "apostles"
required thirty horses to move it. The army carried five
hundred and ten tons of powder.

It is hardly surprising that this royal army, laden with
prefabricated houses, thousands of square feet of marquee,
tons of cloth of gold, mattresses, beds, carpets and hangings,
not to mention the twelve cumbersome "apostles", covered
just three miles before nightfall on its first march out from
Calais! In three days they had covered twelve miles and
St. John the Evangelist lagged further and further behind
until his two and a half tons slipped the harness and fell
into a stream. He was later recovered and returned to the
fold. When Henry's middle-ward eventually puffed its way
to Thérouanne, part of his army had already been sitting
idly around the walls for over a month, waiting for the
siege to begin.

This was to prove a fantastically costly war, but it was
not the cost of the army that strained the exchequer. After
all, a private received only six pence a day, and his "coat
money" for the whole campaign was only two shillings. It
was the extras that swallowed the diminishing treasury re-
serves. The king carried a wardrobe of clothes which he
rarely used more than once, and a velvet gown trimmed with
ermine could cost up to seventeen pounds. Henry trundled
behind him fourteen wagons laden with gold and four with
silver coin. He spent lavishly, giving away gold, jewels and

coins as the whim took him. Two visits to the temporary
residence of Maximillian, the Emperor of Germany, cost
Henry one thousand pound in gifts. To finance this glorious
war, the people at home were severely taxed, and foreign
residents were charged double! But after all, this was the
king's war.

When Henry VIII came to the throne in 1509, he swept
away the careful politics of his father by marrying Catherine
of Aragon, the widow of his brother Arthur. A papal
dispensation was required for this, since the Church had
long decided that the injunction in Leviticus 18: 16, "Thou
shalt not uncover the nakedness of thy brother's wife",
prohibited just such a union as Henry planned. However,
such a dispensation was not hard to obtain if it suited the
pope's convenience, which it did, and if his pocket was
suitably lined, which it was. The young king then proceeded
to sweep away his father's carefully stored fortune with
equal ease. In October 1511, Pope Julius II, "who conducted
the office of pontiff as if he were a sailor on leave", formed
a Holy League with the Emperor of the German States,
Maximillian, and with Ferdinand, King of Spain. It was an
alliance against the growing power of Louis XII of France
and young Henry was so galled at being left out that he
forced his way into the League by offering to attack Louis
in the Spring of 1512. Henry felt himself a sort of Robin
Hood with the pope as the oppressed and Louis as the
Sheriff of Nottingham. He was proud of his new role, but
unfortunately his army was no match for the Sheriff and
Ferdinand failed to provide the promised back up; which
was particularly unfortunate since Ferdinand was the young
king's new father-in-law. This new and kingly invasion of
1513 was designed to wipe out the memory of that disastrous
failure in 1512. He was, after all, the King of England and
France and it was high time the English king asserted his
full title and authority.

THOMAS WOLSEY

But if this was the king's war, it might with equal accuracy
be styled Wolsey's war. Thomas Wolsey was born in 1471,

the year that the Black Death returned to England; and if there was no sinister significance in this, it is certainly true that Wolsey would help Henry to heave England out of the Middle Ages and into the Modern Age. In the two hundred and eighty years before Henry's father came to the throne, England had had twelve kings. Seven of these were deposed (five of them dying violently), two went insane and only three died naturally. Wolsey would ensure that this Henry was here to stay. Unfortunately Henry did not reciprocate the kindly feelings!

Thomas Wolsey was the son of a grazier butcher from Ipswich, yet by 1501 he was chaplain to the Archbishop of Canterbury, and four years later a chaplain to King Henry VII. A man of incredible capacity and stamina he once travelled from Richmond to the Netherlands and back with an urgent dispatch from Henry VII and accomplished the whole journey in less than three days! On another occasion he wrote letters continually from four in the morning for twelve hours. He remained at his post in London long after the sweating sickness had sent the new king and his nobles scurrying into the country.

But Wolsey was drunk with the desire for power, and when the war he engineered in 1512 proved a failure, he stemmed criticism by arranging this new one, which was staged in such a way that it would *look* a brilliant success, whatever the truth of the situation proved to be. Even in 1513 Wolsey, the upstart butcher's son from Ipswich, was second only to the king both in authority and flamboyance, and that fact alone was hardly in keeping with mediaeval codes of nobility. He rose quickly in power, receiving the bishoprics of Tournai and Lincoln, the deanery of the Church of St. Stephens and the Archbishopric of York. He longed to become a cardinal, but not an ordinary cardinal like Warham, the old Archbishop of Canterbury; Wolsey schemed to become a life legate, the pope's personal representative in England. This he achieved in 1525, but when he was created Cardinal in 1515 he made quite sure that all England knew. His cardinal's hat arrived at Dover and when the messenger, arriving in London, failed to

appreciate the importance of his charge, he was sent back to
Dover to transport the hat with due reverence. When it
re-entered London in November, the mayor and
aldermen rode out in full livery to greet it and the
precious object was carried in ceremony to the high altar
where it remained until the Sunday. Even the dukes and
lords bowed to it. On Christmas Eve of the same year
Wolsey became Lord Chancellor of all England.

His splendour knew no bounds. Everywhere he was
preceded by two tall, handsome priests gorgeously clothed
and carrying large crosses; when he journeyed to the Star
Chamber he came "humbly" on a mule which was richly
adorned and with golden stirrups. His power became so
great that the Venetian ambassador once remarked that it
was safer to neglect His Majesty than His Right Reverend
Lordship. And this was ultimately his downfall, for Henry
early determined to be king in his realm. Wolsey acted as a
servant of Rome and a servant of the King of England and
no man, even with red robes, golden crosses and a cardinal's
hat could serve those two masters, a fact that both Wolsey
and his successor Thomas More learnt at the cost of their
lives.

Certainly the most splendid monument to Wolsey's
inordinate pride, fabulous wealth and prodigal extravagance
was Hampton Court Palace. Wolsey was assured that this
was "the most healthy spot within twenty miles of London"
so he took a ninety-nine year lease and set out to dazzle the
eyes of the world with the largest building in England since
the Romans left. In 1515 the Lord Chancellor began his
palace which covered eight acres and contained a thousand
rooms. The furnishings were unbelievably rich. The inventory for the bedrooms alone is incredible: scores upon
scores of beds are listed, of red, green and russet velvet,
satin and silk, with rich curtains and fringes. Sheets were all
silk, blankets, fresh from the looms of Mr Blanket of Bristol,
were soft and white and furred with lamb's wool. The
inventory lists a great bed "for my Lord's own lying". It
had eight mattresses each stuffed with thirteen pounds of
corded wool; there were four pillowcases, two seamed with

black silk and fleurs-de-lys of gold and two with white silk and fleurs-de-lys of red silk. His eminence refused to drink what he called "the diluted sewage" of the Thames water and used two hundred and fifty tons of lead piping to bring fresh water from Coombe Hill, outside Kingston. Over two thousand five hundred people were employed to build the palace and, when finished, more than five hundred were needed to run it, from knights to stable lads. Even the master cook wore velvet and satin with a gold chain round his neck. With silver plate worth one hundred and fifty thousand pounds it is hardly surprising that the banquets held by the pope's personal representative outlavished those of the king himself. In 1527 when Wolsey journeyed out of Calais to conclude an alliance with Francis of France his gentlemen ushers in black coats, with gold chains at their necks, walked three abreast in rank forming a procession three-quarters of a mile long.

THE SIEGE OF THEROUANNE AND TOURNAI

But all this was yet to be. In 1513 Wolsey was the King's Almoner, and the army's master planner who personally supervised everything from the number of tent pegs to the colour of the king's satin robe for each occasion. Henry arrived before Thérouanne at the end of July. The first engagement with the French forces had lasted six hours and by its conclusion only one English soldier and twenty French lay dead on the field; at this rate the whole campaign could last a century! Thérouanne was a strange objective since Boulogne was a natural stronghold and more advantageous. However, once the king had settled himself comfortably into his apartments, no-one would move him – not even King Louis of France who was desperately trying to assemble an army large enough to dislodge the invading force.

In August Maximillian of Germany arrived; it was a time when the English army was not doing well, since there had been virtually no success against the town and Louis was rapidly building his army. So gullible was the young king and so untried in the politics of the sixteenth century that Maximillian, a full member of the Holy League, actually persuaded Henry to pay him twenty thousand pounds plus an allowance of twenty pounds a day for the privilege of having him ride with the English army and providing a few German mercenaries! Henry rode out to meet Maximillian. Resplendent in a coat of cloth of gold, adorned with pearls and precious stones, this massive six foot two inch Henry cut an impressive figure. Nine men at arms carried his helmet and heavy armour; they were dressed in white and crimson and with cloth of gold covered with ornaments. The king's horses were covered with tinkling golden bells that dropped off and were left as souvenirs for the emperor's bodyguard. Unfortunately the weather spoilt the show and the next time Henry and the emperor met it was in the king's house of timber! To the emperor the English camp had the appearance of a small town of tents. All the officers lived splendidly in tents and marquees which were connected to each other by covered passages. Inside the king's marquee, which was covered from floor to roof with cloth of gold, stood a beautiful gilded sideboard with magnificent gold drinking cups.

For all this pomp and show, the real battle was fought and won many miles away at Flodden. Early in September news reached Henry that James IV of Scotland had led his army of forty thousand men across the border in an attempt to relieve the pressure upon his ally Louis XII. The Earl of Surrey marched north with an English force half the size of James's and met the invader at Flodden Edge outside Branxton in Northumberland. By skilful manoeuvering Surrey won the day and left James, an archbishop, two bishops, two abbots, four earls, most of the Scots nobility, and twelve thousand highlanders dead upon the field. Queen Catherine, who had been busy making standards for Surrey's army, rather tactlessly wrote to her husband who was aimlessly whiling away the weeks outside Thérouanne, "This battle hath been to your grace and all your realm the greatest honour that could be, and more than if you should win the Crown of France". This must have galled the king whose only significant battle thus far was won when he himself was a mile or so behind the front line! And even this, the battle of Bomby, or the Battle of the Spurs as history has styled it in honour of the retreating stampede of the French cavalry, was won more by coincidence than strategy.

However, the city obligingly surrendered at nine o'clock on the morning of 23rd August, before the weather turned too cold for the king. Henry rode on to Tournai which, battered by the twelve "apostles", capitulated on 25th September. Unfortunately the ungrateful citizens sullenly refused to accept their new king and when Henry arranged a day of splendid tournaments to convince them of the glory of being English, it poured with typically English rain. The triumphant king decided that with two battles won it was best to return home in case he lost the next round and besides, winter was approaching, the season when kings do not go out to war, even with wooden huts and the twelve "apostles". Thus he put the city in order, packed his wagons and set out for home.

The king returned to a plague-ridden London, a miscarriage by Catherine and measles for himself. By April 1514 Ferdinand of Spain had come to terms with Louis of France, Maximillian of Germany was seeking a truce, even the newly elected pope, Leo X, uncharacteristically did not want war and Henry, who had promised to return to France the following summer, was beginning to look rather a fool. To even things up, the young king, at last realising how the political game was played, signed a treaty with old Louis which, in return for neutrality in the European power struggle and Henry's sister in marriage, brought him in a handsome pension from the King of France. And all this over the heads of Ferdinand, Maximillian and the pope; Henry's political apprenticeship was over.

GOD AND WE

The line of the Tudor Kings had been established on 22nd August, 1485 when the army of Henry's father hacked Richard III to death on the field of Bosworth. The thirty long and bloody years of the War of the Roses between the houses of York and Lancaster were at an end. But the young Henry who succeeded his father in 1509 found it necessary to continue to hack out his security and, to enforce his

authority and religious views, he burned, hanged and
otherwise disposed of a significant proportion of the three
million inhabitants of England and Wales in the sixteenth
century. However, though a tyrant, Henry was not as cruel
as other national leaders of his day. There was a humane
side to Henry and not all who opposed his views had cause
to regret it. When the saintly Dean Colet preached against
this war of 1513, the king did no more than take the priest
for a short stroll and whisper a few words of advice!

But even if Henry steadily depopulated his kingdom until
his own death in 1547, he was nevertheless an attractive
prince who lifted his nation out of the Middle Ages and
shouldered his way into the affairs of the world. When he
died, England was a power to be reckoned with both at sea
and on land and never again could the nation be seen as
one of the pope's distant estates paying exorbitant revenues
to Rome and acting at the beck and call of the pontiff.
Henry was the king who "dragged a nation out of the
Middle Ages, the pope from his throne, and the British
navy from the scrapyard".

Since the year 1213 when King John was excommunicated
and consequently surrendered his kingdom to the pope,
English monarchs had reigned at the behest of the popes.
From that year England paid an annual one thousand
marks (about £666) feudal rent to the See of Rome – until
Henry threw out the landlord in 1534!

Henry VIII was an accomplished sportsman who rode
and hunted well, handled the bow like any gentleman of the
sixteenth century and at tilts and jousts charmed the ladies
with his bravery, skill and physical strength. The king's
parties and tournaments were so frequent that one observer
could be forgiven for commenting, "The King's Majesty is
young and cares for nothing but hunting and girls". He was
an accomplished musician, an able debater, and a writer
whose Latin verse was commended by the literary genius of
the age, Desiderius Erasmus. The king also considered
himself an expert theologian capable of defending the pope
against Martin Luther; this was more conceit than truth,
but his *Assertion of the Seven Sacraments* convinced him that he

was a match for any man in these higher realms and when, for such a spirited attack against Luther, the pope in 1521 conferred upon him the title "Fidei Defensor" (Defender of the Faith), Henry's pride and self confidence knew no bounds. This, more than anything else, contributed to Henry's total commitment to the belief that he was a God-ordained king, and that therefore his every act, with the notable exception of his marriage to Catherine, was impressed with the stamp of divine approval.

With all his abilities, or assumed abilities, the only principle that motivated Henry in his relationship with people was that of expediency. If ever he had tried, as a young king, to be simple and honest, he had been rudely awakened by his war of 1513 and its aftermath. Kings, emperors and popes all broke their words and treaties with the ease of a child plucking daisies in summer. Henry's great attribute was to be a fast and ruthless learner. People, all people, were pawns in his great game of power politics. Henry VIII was, as a little girl once quaintly remarked "a great widower, having lost many wives"! This rapid succession of six wives is the most notable evidence of his ruthlessness. There is no doubt that Henry was genuinely in love with his first wife, Catherine of Aragon. There is equally no doubt that he was infatuated by his second, Anne Boleyn. But he severed his relationship with one by divorce and with the other by the executioner's knife simply because neither could provide him with a male heir to the throne. And *that* Henry must have. Catherine was pregnant eight times in nine years yet produced nothing lasting but a girl, Mary. Certainly he had a son by one of his mistresses, but even Henry found it difficult to see Henry Fitzroy as a future claimant to the throne. Instead he made him Duke of Richmond and Somerset, Lord High Admiral of England, Lord Warden of the Marches and Lord Lieutenant of Ireland – which was not bad for a boy of seven!

In his treatment of his lord chancellors, Henry was no less fickle. Thomas Wolsey, for all his extravagance, was a brilliant administrator; but he made mistakes and the unforgivable crime was that some of these mistakes made

Henry look a fool. Wolsey lied without shame and intrigued without conscience. By 1529 Henry was more than irritated that the pope would not annul his marriage with Catherine, and Wolsey, by now the most hated man in the nation, slipped from favour. Every trouble was blamed upon this most unpopular, conceited, arrogant and flamboyant Holy Father. When he lost the seal of Lord Chancellor and was called to London on the convenient charge of treason, the old man reached the Abbey of St. Mary just west of Leicester and died of fright. On the day of his death, 29th November, 1530 he confessed, "If I had served God as diligently as I have done the king, He would not have given me over in my grey hairs" – and no-one will quarrel with that. Wolsey had outlived his value and by dying of fright he merely saved the king the bother of having him executed.

In Thomas More the king could hardly have found a more contrasting successor to Wolsey. Unlike Wolsey, he was not a priest, yet he was devout and sincere, which Wolsey never was. Long before he gained the office of the Great Seal in October 1529 Thomas More had worn a shirt of hair that drew blood, with the intention of subjecting his passions. Wolsey only wore such a shirt after he had fallen from favour. More lived a relatively frugal life yet when offered five thousand pounds as a reward for writing against Tyndale he refused the reward though he accepted the task.

Thomas More was a sincere and thinking man; in his book *Utopia*, which was the sixteenth century answer to Plato's *Republic*, he longed for the ideal state. But he was also a man blind to the real issues of his day. He made a last-ditch stand against the irresistible advance of reform and tried to retain Henry in the Middle Ages. Thomas More has been called the last great Catholic in England, and so he was. Bitterly and, at times, cruelly opposed to the reformers, the new Chancellor saw religious liberty as the ultimate downfall of Rome in England. In this he was right. He longed for what he called "a perfect uniformity of religion"; anything else would upset the established order; anything else must be vigorously opposed. He later used his masterly literary skills against William Tyndale and hated

Tyndale's English New Testament with a perfect hatred; he called it the "testament of antichrist".

But More was a courageous man and, unlike his predecessor, fright did not kill him before the scaffold. He died for refusing to accept Henry as head of the Church in England; he died a convinced Catholic owning the pope as head of the Church everywhere. Unlike Wolsey, More could claim at his execution, "I die the king's good servant, but God's first", and no-one could argue with the sincerity of that either.

Thomas Cromwell succeeded More as Lord Chancellor. He threw himself into the king's service and wrote his name into every future history book as the man who carried out the king's commission in suppressing the monasteries. With a perfect sense of timing, Henry waited for the last great abbey, at Waltham in Essex, to surrender to the Lord Chancellor in March 1540 before sending Cromwell to the scaffold in July – five years, almost to the day, after Thomas More. Henry thus dispensed with his lord chancellors as easily as he disposed of his wives.

Even the popes became no more than colourful pawns to Henry VIII. It is true that he spent the first half of his reign promoting and protecting the temporal and spiritual power of these Italian princes, but he spent the last half of his reign demolishing it. In fact Henry demolished the power of the pope in England chiefly because the pontiff refused to agree to his divorce of Catherine. The king always wanted things to look legal, regardless of the facts. By June 1533 a Bill took away the pope's right to decide upon matters within the borders of England and thus Convocation was free to declare the marriage void. The pope might excommunicate him, which he did more than once, but the king had proudly given "such a buffet to the pope as he never had before". That Henry was never a Protestant is a plain fact of history, and that he died a convinced adherent to the Roman Catholic faith is equally true. In matters of doctrine Henry lived and died believing Rome was right. His only quarrel was with the temporal power of the pope interfering in the internal affairs of a nation – one of the few acts of

Henry endorsed by history. In November 1534 Henry issued the Act of Supremacy by which His Majesty was to be "accepted and reputed the only Supreme Head on earth of the Church of England . . .". Then followed, in royal language, the outworking of this title: the king would take charge of the Church's religious affairs and finances. Every inmate of every religious house and every person of influence was required to swear allegiance to the Act. Hundreds, including Thomas More and the old and frail Bishop of Rochester, Dr Fisher, refused and died. Two years later the authority of the pope in England was finally dissolved. But the contradictions of his life and religious convictions are seen in the fact that, two days after Cromwell's execution, Henry ordered six people to be hanged, drawn and quartered at Smithfield, three for speaking in favour of the pope and three for holding Protestant views!

The conviction of divine infallibility, which, for Henry VIII if for no-one else, justified the brutal expediency of his policies can best be summed up in his own words. In March 1533 Cranmer was recalled from his post as Ambassador at the Imperial Court in Germany; old Warham had died and Cranmer was to succeed him as Archbishop of Canterbury. Henry would appoint his own Primate of all England, without reference to the pope. "God and We," as Henry immodestly expressed it, ordained Cranmer Primate of all England!

Meanwhile, in the very year that King Henry VIII of England led his circus from the fields of France to the safety of home, William Tyndale was quietly pursuing his studies at the University of Oxford. He could not be aware that his future course would make him the greatest enemy of the king's realm and the object of all the wrath and intrigue that the powerful prince and his lord chancellors could pour upon their opponents. The battle he was to join would prove to be more costly in life, more earnest in prosecution but infinitely more beneficial and significant in the history of the English-speaking people than a thousand wars of the pompous Henry and Wolsey.

CHAPTER 2

TYNDALE AT UNIVERSITY
1508-1521

William Tyndale sat down in the lecture hall in the autumn of 1513 and resigned himself to the monotonous drone of the empty-souled tutor. He did so as a graduate student, having gained his bachelor of arts degree a year earlier. He was now studying for a master's degree which he gained in July 1515.

Tyndale had registered at Magdalen Hall under the name William Hychyns around 1508 when he was only thirteen years of age, although, since Magdalen Hall was more of a grammar school attached to the college than a university college itself, this young age was by no means unusual. Hychyns was the name assumed by the family when they had fled south from the dale (valley) of the Tyne in Northumberland during the Wars of the Roses. When the Lancastrian house was gaining ground, many families changed their name and tried to start a new life away from their old home. The first Hychyn is found in the West Country in 1478, but by 1520 the family had reverted to its original name of Tyndale. Something of the outlaw and exile was already flowing in the veins of William Hychyns.

Just where and when Tyndale was born is impossible to tell, but it may be supposed that he was born about the year 1494, since a student was not allowed to gain his master's degree before the age of twenty and, according to the university records, "William Hychyns" became master in 1515. We may also claim with some certainty that he was born in the Slymbridge area of Gloucestershire from a

family of well-to-do yeomen farmers. Tyndale families were
certainly living in Melksham Court at Stinchcombe and at
Southend Farm in the village of Southend by the end of the
fifteenth century. What is more certain still is the fact that
Edward Tyndale took over the lease of Hurst Farm at
Slymbridge in 1516 and, according to a letter written in
1533 by Stokesley, the Bishop of London, he was "brother to
Tyndale the archheretic". There was also another brother,
John, and both were greatly influenced by William; in later
years John was fined for distributing Bibles and Edward
left a number of prohibited books in his will. But none of
this certainly fixes the birthplace of William, which is not
inappropriate for the man who became the "Scarlet Pimpernel" of the sixteenth century.

THE SIXTEENTH CENTURY STUDENT

Tyndale's mind was keen and alert and he threw himself
into his studies. The preliminary arts course consisted of
grammar, arithmetic, geometry, astronomy, the theory of
music, rhetoric, logic and philosophy. The students learned
most things by rote, but a rigorous oral debate had to be
successfully undertaken before graduation. After three years
another test could earn the master's degree, but meanwhile
the graduate must lecture on the philosophy of Aristotle. For
the student at Oxford or Cambridge (and there were no
other universities in the country) it was at least eight years
before lectures were given on the Bible. Tyndale could
rightly complain in later years that at the time of gaining
his first degree he had to swear to "hold none opinion
condemned by the Church"; but since at that time he had
never once been lectured on Scripture or doctrine, no
student could know what opinions the Church held or
condemned. Tyndale himself revealed the contradictions
and folly of this teaching system when in 1528 he wrote in
The Obedience of a Christian Man, "When they have thiswise
brawled eight, ten or twelve or more years, and after that
their judgements are utterly corrupt, then they begin their
divinity; not at the scripture, but every man taketh a sundry

doctor; which doctors are as sundry and as divers, the one contrary unto the other, as there are divers fashions and monstrous shapes, none like another, among our sects of religion. Every religion, every university, and almost every man, hath a sundry divinity . . . and every man, to maintain his doctor withal corrupteth the scripture, and fashioneth it after his own imagination, as a potter doth his clay".

When these lectures were eventually given, they followed one of the schools of church fathers: Thomas Aquinas, Duns Scotus and many others, and the interpretation of Scripture at this period was often bordering upon the ridiculous. According to Erasmus, the scholastic teachers used their time in debating such issues as, "Can God produce an infinite in all directions? . . . Could He have made the world better than it is? . . . Can He create a universal which has no particulars? . . . Can He make a thing done not to have been done? . . . Can He make a harlot into a virgin? . . . Can the pope command angels? . . . Is the pope more merciful than Christ?" and so on, with hundreds of such questions seriously debated by the theologians. "Over speculations like these," concluded Erasmus, "theologians professing to teach Christianity have been squandering their lives." This was the useless type of theology to which Tyndale was exposed at Oxford. The Realists, Nominalists, Thomists, Albertists, Occamists, Scotists were "all so learned that an apostle would have no chance with them in argument". Such vainglory made Erasmus scholastically sick. Let no-one suggest that the Church was a glorious unity of belief spoilt only by the reformers!

However, if the lectures were dull and monotonous the university was alive with an air of excitement and discovery. There may have been scholastic hair-splitting in the lecture hall, but in the corridors and narrow streets the students were thinking and debating. And none more than William Hychyns. It was the age of the Renaissance; with the revival of learning and culture, literature and art were establishing their importance in men's minds. It was the great age of art with such men as Michaelangelo and Raphael, and of the discovery of new lands following upon the voyages of Columbus and Cabot. For years the universities had been declining and noblemen considered it a disgrace to send their sons to the so-called halls of learning; at least one expressed his preference to see his sons hanged as criminals rather than go to university. A gentleman's education lay in the hunt and at the dance. But change was in the air. Scholars were becoming the pets of kings and nobles; men boasted of their ability with letters, and the college students began to talk freely. Some credit for this must be given to Erasmus and some even to Henry VIII, but behind it all was an unseen hand preparing England for the greatest reformation she would ever see.

Two hundred years before William arrived at Oxford, Walter Burley, at Merton College, recommended a return to the study of the Scriptures, and disputed the scholastic approach; but he was far ahead of his time. Then John Wycliffe came to Oxford, became a don, Master of Balliol College by 1360 and received his doctorate in 1371. Wycliffe put Burley into practice and eventually provided England with its first translation of the Bible in the common tongue. It is true that the original languages of Hebrew and Greek were unknown to him and that he therefore translated from the Latin Vulgate, but nevertheless his translation from a translation was a valuable start. Handwritten copies circulated as fast as they could be produced. Wycliffe died in 1384 at Lutterworth, a short riding distance from Oxford. Condemned by the pope but protected by John of Gaunt, Duke of Lancaster, Wycliffe involved Oxford in the great struggle for freedom of thought and a return to Scripture. "Are we then the very dregs of humanity," roared Lancaster in 1390 when the House of Lords was presented with a motion to seize and burn all the copies of Wycliffe's Bibles, "that we cannot possess the laws of our religion in our own tongue?" Apparently we were, for attempts to stamp out Wycliffe's "Poor Preachers" or "Lollards" as they became known, went on well into the fifteenth century. Oxford reacted strongly against this intrusion into its scholastic slumber; freedom of thought and wide thinking were discouraged, true scholarship was ridiculed.

THE INFLUENCE OF THE NEW LEARNING

Then in 1483 Dean Colet came to Oxford, a saintly scholar who later became Dean of St. Paul's London and who ought to have gone to the scaffold for his outspoken views. Colet soon began lectures upon the letter of Paul to the Romans. This man who "taught and lived like St. Paul" drew many to hear him. Colet never advocated one change in the doctrines of the Church of Rome, but his sermons against the corrupt practices of the Church, and his reforms when he was Dean of St. Paul's, led the Bishop of London to clamour for his death.

In 1497 another great and pious scholar slipped in from the continent and became a life-long friend of Colet. Desiderius Erasmus was born at Rotterdam in 1467 and became the greatest literary scholar of the sixteenth century. He was working hard to grasp the Greek language and master the many Greek manuscripts that had recently arrived in the west when Constantinople fell to the Turkish armies on 29th May, 1453. When Erasmus arrived in Oxford his writings had already preceded him and he was climbing the ladder of fame. Colet, Erasmus and Grocyn, who had recently begun lectures in Greek, spent hours together and Erasmus soon reported that he could make a tolerable bow and smile graciously whether he meant it or not. He was becoming all that was required of an English gentleman!

However valuable his stay at Oxford, it was at Cambridge that Erasmus made his greatest contribution. In 1511 he came to Cambridge to lecture in Greek; he was appointed to the Lady Margaret chair of Divinity, stayed for three years and hated every minute of it. It was the time of Henry's war and consequently a time of soaring inflation. "All articles have gone up in price," he lamented, "and the bad wine gives me the stone". Nothing could be worse for a homesick exile than inflation and gall stones! In addition, the mists and frosts drifting across the Cambridge fen country and the chilly opposition of the dons to the new learning made this poor scholar long for the sunshine and great libraries of Rome. But it was here that Erasmus was working hard to compile his Greek New Testament. The scholastics railed and stormed. It was the devil's own language, and arch-heresy (everything you disagreed with in the sixteenth century was heresy, even Greek!); the prelates raised an eyebrow, it could be dangerous, but since the ploughman could not read Greek any more than Latin, the danger seemed minimal. The students bought it and studied it. Erasmus stayed on to lecture.

Erasmus left Cambridge well before 1519, the year in which Tyndale transferred his allegiance from Oxford and moved to the university in the fen country, but his influence was still felt there. Oxford had had its opportunity with Wycliffe, and Cambridge became the university of the reformers. Names like Gardiner, Ridley, Bilney, Latimer, Cranmer, Barnes, Coverdale, Frith, Parker, Grindal, Whitgift and others, are all found in the Cambridge register. There were probably two things that attracted William Tyndale to Cambridge. The first was undoubtedly the influence of Erasmus and his Greek New Testament. Tyndale had read all that Erasmus had written and it closely matched his own thinking. William also had a passion for learning and languages, and he was hard at work to master Greek. This language was now well entrenched at Cambridge and all the serious students were reading and discussing the Greek New Testament. Tyndale poured over it and expended his precious pennies to read it late into the night. With a preface to each book, and notes, liberally and vigorously applied to the state of the Church, it is one of the astonishing facts of history that such a book circulated with the blessing of the pope. The effect of this book was startling. Thomas Bilney, a graduate of Trinity Hall, was one of many deeply affected by the Greek New Testament. He heard a group of men discussing it and became so intrigued that he purchased a copy and began reading in Paul's letters. There he read, "This is a true saying and by all means worthy to be received, that Christ Jesus came into the world to save sinners". He was so transformed from his depressing sense of guilt that he could record, "I seemed unto myself inwardly to feel a marvellous comfort and quietness insomuch that my bruised bones leaped for joy". For this faith Bilney died at the stake in the Lollard's pit, under St. Leonard's Hill, Norwich on 19th August, 1531.

It was such men as Bilney who formed the second attraction for Tyndale to move to Cambridge. Soon after his arrival the Oxford graduate found himself walking along King's Parade towards the White Horse Inn where, over their small beer, an earnest group of young men discussed and debated the great issues of the Scriptures and Church doctrines. As in every path of his future life, Tyndale left little record of his stay anywhere and we may imagine him listening quietly and forming his own views. Tyndale was an independent man and would be stamped in no mould but that of the Scriptures. His views were by no means fixed as yet and he was not a man, like some of the zealous young reformers, to shout about that which he did not fully grasp. His friends must often have sought his counsel, for his few words were well considered and balanced. Certainly they could not but admire his life and simple consistency. There were no contradictions in the life of William Tyndale. Years later in 1529 Sir Thomas More, the most bitter opponent of Tyndale, acknowledged that he was "as men say, well known, before he went over the sea, for a man of right good living, studious and well learned in Scripture, and in divers places in England was very well liked, and did great good with preaching . . . (he was) taken for a man of sober and honest living, and looked and preached holily". Tyndale had been ordained whilst at Oxford in 1514 but, though this gave him the right to preach, he determined never to enter monastic orders.

But this new learning and its dangerous views were not unnoticed by the authorities. By 1520 Archbishop Warham warned Chancellor Wolsey that he had read letters from Oxford "stating that the university is infected with Lutheranism", and the Cardinal made a pompous inspection of the city. Many banned books were circulating. The following year attempts were made to stem the tide and Tyndale doubtless stood with his companions at a discreet distance

to watch the massive bonfire of prohibited books outside the
west door of Great St. Mary's Church.

THE SIXTEENTH CENTURY CHURCH

To say that the Church in which Tyndale was brought up
was corrupt and disgraceful is not a statement of blind
prejudice but one of sad historical fact. The Church of Rome
by the time of Tyndale was, and had been for centuries,
rotten from the head downwards. Certainly this was admitted by some of the most influential men of the day, but they
were voices crying in the wilderness and were themselves
caught in the very trap of which they bitterly complained.
Unlike the evangelical reformers, they had no effective
answer to the sickness.

In the fifteenth century Archbishop Morton had lamented
the state of the Church and urged the pope to correct some
of the obvious abuses, but nothing was effectively done.
Dean Colet, Thomas More and Erasmus were all men who
lived and died in the bosom of the Church and never
touched the authority of the pope, the doctrines of the
Church, or the supremacy of the Catholic faith; Thomas
More went to the scaffold in defence of all this. From such
men we may learn the state of the Church at the time of
Tyndale.

With the corrupt election in 1492 of Rodrigo Borgia as
Pope Alexander VI the transition from the Middle Ages
to the Modern Age began disastrously. For the next few
decades the papacy was, as the Roman historian Father
Bede Jarrett admits, "little else than a small Italian prince-
dom ruled by some of the least reputable of the Renaissance
princes". The early life of this pope was, in keeping with the
nobility of the day, a shameful scandal; during his period of
office he spent much of his time granting benefices to his
illegitimate children. In 1497 a Bill of Reform was issued
which admitted that in the Church "licentiousness has
reached an intolerable pitch". The list of reforms necessary,
including the prohibition of simony, keeping concubines,
and solemn vows by children, reveal the state of the Church,
but the Bill never succeeded beyond the draft state and was

soon forgotten. Archbishop Morton could go on complaining. Even the great Roman Catholic historian, Dr Ludwig Pastor, admits of Alexander, "His life of unrestrained sensuality was in direct contradiction with the precepts of Him whose representative on earth he was".

Julius II reigned from 1503 and died shortly after Henry brought his "circus" back from France in 1513. According to a contemporary Venetian Ambassador he was violent, impetuous and untrustworthy. A giant in body and passions, "his language overstepped all due bounds in its rudeness and violence", a fault which increased as he grew older. Julius, according to Pastor, was more like a warrior than a pope, yet he was the saviour of the papacy and his threats of excommunication and his use of the sword guaranteed that by his death the Kingdom of St. Peter included the best and richest portions of Italy. In 1506 Julius began his work on the magnificent monument to extortion in the form of St. Peter's Cathedral in Rome. To finance it he issued a Plenary Indulgence which guaranteed that on payment of a fee, a diploma of pardon could be received.

Leo X followed Julius, having become a monk at seven and a cardinal at fourteen! In unparalleled double-dealing he signed a treaty with France in January 1519 for mutual defence just three days after secretly signing a similar treaty with Charles V of Spain. King Henry had some good examples to follow from the Holy Father in his own political manoeuvering. Leo increased the sales of indulgences to such an extent that even Cardinal Ximenes, whose devotion to the Church of Rome ranked second to none, protested. But Leo needed money.

The Church was barely even religious. A contemporary commented, "The clergy are to be found in inns and taverns, and at sports and theatres, more frequently than in consecrated places". Leo raised money by any and every means. He sold indulgences, created new offices and sold them to the highest bidder and enjoyed card-playing and the coarse jests of his courtiers. He spent at least one month each year hunting on his estates and arranged festivities that exceeded in extravagance those of Wolsey and Henry

combined. At the time of Martin Luther's heroic stand at
the Diet of Worms in 1521, Leo was at St. Angelo watching
an irreverent and indecent play concerning a young woman,
Venus, Cupid and seven lovers. He ignored Luther, Tyndale,
the Turks and the immense problems of Europe, having
preference for his artists, poets, musicians, actors and
buffoons. On his death it was claimed that "Leo has eaten
up three Pontificates: the treasury of Julius II, the revenues
of his own Pontificate, and those of his successor". Even
such sympathy as Pastor can give stretches our credulity:
"Certainly he was no unbeliever, even though he was not a
man of deep interior religion"!

Adrian VI succeeded in 1521 but he was too sincere and
saintly for Rome and died within twelve months. Clement
VII was tall, good-looking, modest and chaste in his living
but sadly incompetent, losing more battles than any pope.
On 7th May, 1527 Rome was sacked by merciless German
troops and Clement was twice a prisoner of his own Catholic
subjects.

In 1534 Pope Paul III came to power, his three illegitimate
children having been earlier legitimised by Julius II. But
we need look at the head no longer. We know that if the
head is sick then the whole body is full of sores.

Yet in spite of this terrible state of affairs all Europe still
believed passionately that the pope and his councils could
not err. They accepted without question the teaching concerning the unbroken line of apostolic succession from the
Apostle Peter onwards. Even history made nonsense of this,
and the reformers were not slow to point to the many contradictory statements of successive popes and to the occasional historical embarrassments. In 1378, for example, there
were two popes. Urban VI lived at Rome, and Clement VII
at Avignon. Since each had excommunicated the other, who
could tell the true successor to Peter? This state of affairs
continued until the French king and the body of cardinals
ordered the two successors of Urban and Clement to
appear at a general council in 1409. They refused, and to
save further trouble the council deposed both and elected
Alexander V, who promptly deposed the council. But now

there were three popes! Alexander reduced the problem to its original proportion by dying within a year and John XXIII succeeded. But everyone knew that His Holiness John XXIII had been a former pirate and he was soon imprisoned for his nefarious deeds. Of the remaining two popes Gregory XII abdicated in 1415 and Benedict XIII held out until 1417. Now, with no pope at all, the schism was neatly healed after nearly forty years, and Martin V was elected. But it was taxing the ability of the ablest historian and the credulity of the most credulous saint to understand what had happened to the unbroken line of apostolic succession in all these manoeuvres.

IGNORANCE, RELICS AND CORRUPTION

Certainly Erasmus and others cried in alarm and tried to sting the authorities into action. Erasmus had been forced to take monastic vows when he was in his teens but early determined "to live wholly to God, to repent of the sins of my foolish youth, to study the scriptures and to read or write something of real value. I could do nothing of this in a convent". Erasmus was a scholar devoted to his books and learning, but there was little real scholarship in his day. He was devastating in his criticism of what went on in the halls of learning. "Theology itself I reverence and always have reverenced," he wrote. "I am speaking merely of the theologastrics of our own time, whose brains are the rottenest, intellects the dullest, doctrines the thorniest, manners the brutalest, life the foulest, speech the spitefulest, hearts the blackest that I have ever encountered in the world." If this was true, and all the thinking world knew that it was, then it is little wonder that men produced by the monasteries and colleges were too frequently blind and lazy fools at best. The pious Dean Colet was as scathing as Erasmus: "O priests! O priesthood! O the detestable impiety of those miserable priests, of whom this age of ours contains a great multitude, who fear not to rush from the bosom of some foul harlot into the temple of the church, to the altar of Christ, to the mysteries of God! Abandoned creatures, on whom the vengeance of God will one day fall the heavier, the more shamelessly they have intruded themselves on the divine office." The language of the evangelical reformers never exceeded this.

Deplorable though this was, the case of the priests who could barely read was hardly less tragic. All over Europe, and England in particular, priests mumbled through services in a Latin that they did not understand. As long before as 1281 Archbishop Peckham lamented, "The ignorance of the priests casteth the people into the ditch of error". Nothing had been done to change the position, and the country lay under a dark pall of superstition and ignorance. Everywhere friars travelled with their holy relics which, for a fee, could be viewed and kissed. In Germany, in the city of Martin Luther, at Wittenberg in Saxony, the Castle Church contained over seventeen thousand relics including part of the rock on which Jesus stood when He wept over Jerusalem, the gown of the virgin Mary and some milk from her breasts, a piece from the burning bush of Moses, thirty-five portions of the cross, hay and straw from the manger at Bethlehem, some hair from Christ, His coat and girdle, and even a complete skeleton of one of the babes murdered by Herod at Bethlehem! The Elector of Saxony was proud of his collection. This was an Indulgence Church, and the pilgrim could earn one hundred and twenty-seven thousand seven hundred and nine years and one hundred and sixteen days off purgatory by viewing them all; as a bonus he helped to increase the Church revenues.

During 1514 Erasmus and Colet visited the relics at Canterbury. At the shrine of St. Thomas à Becket, Erasmus shuddered at the gruesome articles reverently handed to him: "An amazing quantity of bones: skulls, jawbones, teeth, hands, fingers, whole arms, all which we adoringly kissed," and he noted that when an arm with bleeding flesh hanging from it was offered to a companion by the name of Gratian, he visibly recoiled. Neither Gratian nor Erasmus was impressed, but the plain Englishman was. He believed everything. He believed that the taper held in the arms of Our Lady in the Benedictine Priory at Cardigan had once burned for nine years without consuming the wood; he was so certain of the

claim that whoever offered anything to the image of Darvel
Gatheren in Wales would find that he had power to fetch
him out of hell, that five hundred pilgrims visited the image
in one day. Not until the commissioners of Thomas Cromwell
entered the Cistercian Abbey at Boxley in Kent were the
villagers reliably informed that no miracle occurred when
the image of the virgin smiled or frowned at their gifts but
that "a system of wires and pulleys cunningly hidden caused
her eyes and lips to move . . .". At Hayles Abbey in Gloucester a crystal vessel contained the blood of Christ. This blood
was supposedly invisible to the impenitent and visible only
when absolution, on payment of a fee, was granted. In fact
the priests merely turned a thick side of the glass to the
penitent until sufficient money had been paid. Even Thomas
More scoffed at the London women praying before the
image of Our Lady, just by the Tower of London, "till each
of them believes it is smiling upon her". But *nothing* was
ever done to change this tragic state of affairs. Why should
it be? From birth to death the people were immersed in
superstition and this was the greatest means of Church
revenue. Unquestioning obedience to the Church was
demanded and the fearful spectre of excommunication held
everyone from king to ploughman in servile obedience.

The lives of the clergy defy description. Erasmus declared,
"No word of Christ is heard in the pulpits"; and again, "I
doubt whether in the whole history of Christianity the heads
of the Church have been so grossly worldly as at the present
moment". According to the Royal Commissioners as late as
1538 these were understatements. At the Abbey of Wardon
in Berkshire "brothel women" were regular visitors and the
brothers were "common drunkards". The Abbot of the
large Benedictine Abbey at Bury St. Edmunds "delighted
much in playing in dice and cards, and therein spent much
money". At Hounslow the Trinitarian monks were heavily
in debt to the townsfolk and by common report they "drink
weekly all the town dry . . . and yet when they were most
drunk at night and (were) led home to their house by the
inhabitants there, then the same self persons were most holy
in the morning, and most ready to sing mass. . . ." At an

abbey in Wiltshire the prior had six children. And why not?
Nearly all the popes had children and Thomas Wolsey, the
pope's representative in England, when he was almoner to
the king, lived at Bridewell House with his "wife", whom he
later gave to one George Legh of Aldington – complete with
dowry! Wolsey's daughter was put in a convent and his son
was given a Church benefice at the age of ten. Even Archbishop Warham of Canterbury had such a "wife". All the
world knew of this and none hated it more than Erasmus and
Colet. Nor was it anything new. Before 1490 Archbishop
Morton of Canterbury had charged the great Abbey of
St. Albans with having "laid aside the pleasant yoke of
contemplation and all regular observance, alms, and other
offices of piety". He accused the abbot of having appointed
as prioress "a woman who had already married, and who
lived in adultery with the monks. . . ." The brothers of the
Abbey, Morton continued, "live with harlots and mistresses
publicly and continuously within the precincts of the
monastery". The abbot dined in state, and in serving him
at his table raised fifteen steps above the rest, the monks
chanted a hymn at every fifth step. The situation at Norwich
and elsewhere, according to Morton, was no better. By the
time Tyndale arrived at Cambridge even Wolsey, ignoring
his own worldly life, set out to visit the monasteries with the
intention of imposing a little reform.

It was the age of pluralities, the owning of numerous
"livings" which were rarely, if ever visited. The cardinal or
bishop would take the lion's share of the income and pass the
living to a priest lower down the scale. At the bottom of the
ladder the poor, ignorant curate was left in charge and paid
a pittance. Wolsey was at one and the same time Bishop of
Tournai, Bishop of Lincoln, Dean of the Chapter of St.
Stephens and Archbishop of York – and he was only just
commencing his spectacular career at this time. Even pious
Colet was Dean of St. Paul's in London, rector of a parish in
Suffolk, prebendary of the Cathedrals of York and Salisbury
and treasurer of Chichester Cathedral – and he later added
to these. Tyndale's own county of Gloucestershire was a
stronghold of the Church, with six mitred abbeys and

numerous priories, monasteries, convents and cells. For fifty years Italian bishops held the livings of Gloucester and Worcester and it is doubtful if any of them ever visited England. The ninety monasteries in Gloucestershire owned sixty-five thousand acres of land.

But let anyone complain at all this and it was the worse for him. The Church was above the law. By ancient right the state could never interfere in the life of the cleric, however low his station or however great his crime. He could murder, steal or seduce the Lord of the Manor's wife, and if the bishop granted him absolution then the matter rested there. Psalm 51: 1 became ridiculed as the "neck-verse"; provided the ignorant cleric could stumble through it in Latin he proved his right to trial by the Church court alone. Only when the Church turned over one of its members to the secular powers could punishment be offered. The popes claimed nations and empires and distributed them at will. They controlled kings and princes and ordered them as they wished. Although Rome never had legal authority over either Church or state in England that did not stop her claiming such. Pope Adrian gave the whole of Ireland to Henry II, King of England, in the twelfth century, provided he could conquer it! The resulting conflict between the Church and state over such a monopoly is not hard to imagine, and it was largely this state of affairs that Henry VIII set out to correct. This situation was partly offset by an Act of Parliament in 1512 but it is always easier to pass an act than to implement it.

Such was the religious state of Tyndale's world. It is neither useful nor seemly to describe it in more detail. Attempts have been made to defend the position. The great Catholic leader of the last century, Cardinal Newman, referred to this view of the Church as built upon wholesale, unscrupulous lying; a less capable mind more recently admitted that occasionally monks or nuns were not all that they should be, "but only bigots determined to blacken the Roman Catholic religion would assert more than this today". If this is so then some of the noblest minds of the Roman Church – Archbishop Morton, Dean Colet, Sir

Thomas More, and Desiderius Erasmus, must be dismissed as unscrupulous liars and determined bigots – but it is a little too easy to avoid the truth in this way. None of the evangelical reformers, not even excepting Luther, used such fierce and condemning language and such wide-sweeping judgements as Erasmus did in his play "Julius II Exclusus", in which he pictured the pope denied access to heaven in spite of his railing at Peter. The play was such a masterpiece that it was an instant success in Paris in 1514.

Tyndale watched his world, listened to debates and read Erasmus. He loved Erasmus for the stark truth of his statements and the fine style of his Latin prose. But he loved him more for his Greek New Testament. William Tyndale wrestled with the Book which had so recently come into his possession. The notes added by Erasmus fitted the case so well. By Matthew 19: 13 Tyndale read, "Men are threatened or tempted into vows of celibacy. They can have license to go with harlots, but they must not marry wives. They may keep concubines and remain priests. If they take wives they are thrown to the flames". Beside Matthew 23: 27 he read, "What would Jerome say could he see the virgin's milk exhibited for money, with as much honour paid to it as to the consecrated body of Christ; the miraculous oil; the portions of the true cross, enough if they were collected to freight a large ship? Here we have the hood of St. Francis, there Our Lady's petticoat or St. Anne's comb, or St. Thomas of Canterbury's shoes; not presented as innocent aids to religion, but as the substance of religion itself . . ." And by Matthew 24: 23, "I saw with my own eyes Pope Julius II at Bologna, and afterward at Rome, marching at the head of a triumphal procession as if he were Pompey or Caesar. St. Peter subdued the world with faith, not with arms or soldiers or military engines . . ." On the unknown tongues of 1 Corinthians 14: 19 Erasmus wrote bitterly of the pre-occupation with singing: "Money must be raised to buy organs and train boys to squeal. . . . They have so much of it in England that the monks attend to nothing else. A set of creatures who ought to be lamenting their sins fancy they can please God by gurgling in their throats. . . ."

But the more Tyndale read on, the more dissatisfied he became. It was not the Greek Text that troubled him, he would not presume to improve upon that. It was not even those apt and searching comments of Erasmus that caused his concern. For a man as honest as Tyndale they married only too well with the life he saw all around him. It was what the great Dutch scholar did not say that left a void, an incompleteness, in his own thinking. Erasmus ably exposed the running sores of Rome, but he never probed to the root cause of the wound; he had no real diagnosis or remedy. Surely there was more to be said.

Tyndale realised he must get away from Cambridge. It was not the growing opposition to Lutheranism that forced him out, he was made of bolder stuff than that. But if he was going to fight a corrupt system he must know his ground more surely and discover how best he could serve the Lord who had died for him. Cambridge was all talk, argument, debate; it was all hurry and gossip. Young men were eager to enter the battle of words but Tyndale knew it would not end with words only. Many of these zealous young men would recant, conform, and "carry the faggot" to a pile of burning heretical books before they found courage to die for their faith. Tyndale was a more decisive man. He would follow no crowd blindly, even if the crowd was moving vaguely in the right direction. He must get away to think, and pray and study the New Testament more. With a mind as clear and able as his, the halls of learning and the path of renown were open to him; but the Spirit of God was drawing him in another direction.

CHAPTER 3

LITTLE SODBURY MANOR
1521-1523

A servant slipped from the Great Hall in response to the announcement of the arrival of a visitor, pushed the massive wooden bolt into its three foot cavity in the wall and swung open the heavy oak door. The young priest needed little introduction. His brother, Edward, was well known in the county of Gloucestershire and the family home of the Tyndales was not more than a dozen miles to the south. William carried his few belongings to the attic room set apart for his use, hurriedly shook the dust from his clothes and went downstairs to meet his new master, Sir John Walsh.

Sir John was a young man of about thirty-five years; he was an important figure in the county and had had the distinction of acting as the king's Champion at Henry's Coronation in 1509. He was later to act twice as High Sheriff of Gloucestershire and in 1535, when Tyndale was in very different circumstances, entertained the king and Anne Boleyn at his manor. Sir John had prudently married Anne Poyntz, the daughter of a notable Gloucester family. Sir John and Lady Walsh had two sons, the elder of whom was only six when Tyndale arrived, and the two small boys were formally ushered into the Hall to meet their new tutor.

Little Sodbury Manor was built on a terrace on the side of a Cotswold hill. The small manor house came into the possession of the Walsh family in 1491 and Sir John's father made a number of alterations and additions which gave the manor a distinctly uneven and unplanned appearance inside. Outside, the grey Cotswold stone walls and stone

"Little Sodbury Manor" Tyndale's home in 1521-1522

tiled roof defied the strong winds, whipping across the
Severn Valley, to pluck the little manor from its perch on
the side of the hill. William surveyed the Great Hall with its
tall oak-beamed ceiling, wooden screens at the south end
towards the main door, and oak panelled walls. He noticed
the massive fire place on the north wall, the black and white
mosaic floor and the long, heavy oak table in the centre.
The young scholar from Cambridge was unaware that some
of his earliest contests would be fought at this table and that
seated here he would make public a decision that even now
was forcing its way into his heart and mind, a decision that
would change the face of England.

In addition to the not very onerous task of teaching the
two boys to read, write and count, Tyndale preached in the
little church of St. Adeline, the only church of that name in
England, which perched precariously above the manor.
Each Sunday Sir John and his family mounted the stone
steps immediately behind the manor, walked between the
two old yew trees which stood sentinel before the church
door, and gathered in the family pew; the peasant farmers
and servants filled the small chapel and stood, lounged or
sat on the floor whilst Tyndale entered his plain wooden
pulpit, carved after the fashion of the manor house panelling,
and expounded the Scriptures simply and forcefully. But
he was not officially chaplain, nor did he have the charge
of the village at the foot of the hill. So at Little Sodbury
Manor Tyndale found time to think and study. The room
chosen for him was quiet and as far away from the boys and
noises of the home as was possible in a small manor. His
room was on the third floor and the steep arched ceiling, the
eaves of which fell almost to the floor, was made of ships'
timbers from the Avonmouth. Tyndale would often meet
poor redundant or crippled sailors from nearby Bristol,
begging for sixpence in the surrounding countryside. A small
stone-framed window on the south-east looked out upon his
little church. If Tyndale stepped outside the door and up a
flight of five stairs to a tiny turret-room, he faced an almost
breathtaking view across the Severn Vale. The quiet,
thoughtful scholar required little more than a bed, a table

and chair, and a small cupboard for his few personal belongings. On cold days he worked by the large stone fireplace, whilst in the summer he would doubtless sit at the window to catch as much light as possible and use every day-light hour to full advantage.

Tyndale translated into English a work by Erasmus called the *Manual of the Christian Soldier*. This little book, written in 1502, described the spiritual armour of the Christian Knight, and the rules by which he should order his life. Erasmus urged the reader to study the Scriptures and the book abounded in quotations from the Word of God. Tyndale courteously presented a copy of his translation to Sir John and Lady Walsh and they were clearly proud of their tutor's scholarship and impressed by his serious and gracious way of life. Meanwhile, the quiet tutor pressed on with his studies and mastered a number of languages. The humanist[1] Buschius met him on the continent five years later and reported Tyndale's skill in seven languages, including Hebrew.

CAMP HILL

It was probably mid-summer 1521 when Tyndale arrived at Little Sodbury Manor and on many warm afternoons he must have climbed to Camp Hill, situated just above the little church. Here, while the boys ran about, the sheep pulled lazily at the grass, and the noisy jackdaws chattered and squabbled around the stone church, William could sit down and look over the scene in front of him. It was not only beautiful in the extreme, but it framed a miniature of the whole of so-called Christendom. Far on the western horizon William could make out the Welsh hills and before them, spread out to the very foot of Camp Hill, lay the plains of the Severn Valley. His eyes wandered across the common lands, woods, and meadows. The villages dotted the plain

---

[1] Humanism at this time was not anti-religious. Throughout the Middle Ages man's life on earth was seen as of importance only insofar as it affected his welfare after death. The sixteenth century Renaissance, on the other hand, asserted the value of man's potential on earth. Thus Erasmus, a fervent churchman, was quite properly one of the greatest humanists of his day. Atheistic humanism was not known at this time.

with their poor houses. Most of the homes were so simple
that they were little more than two large curved pieces of
oak with a ridge pole between them. Wattle-and-daub (a
mixture of clay, dung and straw) completed the walls of
this tent-like structure. Even with good, solid Cotswold
stone around few houses used it; that was reserved for the
manor. Chimneys were a recent innovation and although
most homes at least now poked a hole in the roof the grand-
parents bitterly complained at the ridiculous way to relieve
the smoky atmosphere, and as late as 1550 one lord considered chimneys effeminate!

Glass was unknown to the village home. A peasant's home
might have two rooms, the bower and the hall. In the
bower, the family was born, slept and died; in the hall
everything else happened. A few scrawny hens scratched
among the straw-covered floor, the family's two lean hogs
snorted and rooted inside and outside and perhaps a cow
was tethered nearby and allowed in during the long cold
winter nights. Few families could afford either wax or
tallow for lights. Utensils were of the simplest and most
homes managed with a few earthenware bowls and a brass
or iron cooking pot; two tree stumps and a plank made an
adequate table. With the dirty and insanitary life of the
peasant, death was a familiar figure at the door of every
home; Dean Colet was the only survivor of twenty-two
children. Since the village priest demanded the best article
of the deceased, life was a constant fight against poverty. It
is true that England was painfully heaving itself out of the
serfdom of the Middle Ages. The rebellions of Wat Tyler in
1381 and Jack Cade in 1450 had revealed a peasantry ready
to assert itself; and these peasant revolts, together with a
boom in the wool trade, all made for some improvements
in the standards of living. But still the peasant's life was hard
and he was well aware of the effect of the curse upon Adam's
sin: "Cursed is the ground for thy sake; in sorrow shalt
thou eat of it all the days of thy life; thorns also and thistles
shall it bring forth to thee; and thou shalt eat the herb of
the field; in the sweat of thy face shalt thou eat bread, till
thou return unto the ground; for out of it wast thou taken:

for dust thou art, and unto dust shalt thou return" (Genesis 3: 17-19).

The peasant was allotted strips of land and each house had its own small garden. If he was lucky he might be allowed a twenty-acre strip on which he could earn himself thirty-five shillings a year. But an ox cost thirteen shillings in the market and he needed two for his plough. Towards the autumn Tyndale could watch the scores of ploughmen driving the yoke of oxen or pair of horses up and down these strips. His eyes stopped roving the plain as he fastened upon a ploughman. John Ploughman was the symbol of the hard-working, ignorant, superstitious and desperately poor country Englishman. No-one cared for him and he was imprisoned in his village. It was virtually unknown for the ploughman to become anything else. Tyndale and all the scholars had the Bible in Latin and now the New Testament in Greek, but what use was that to the man behind the plough? How could the Latin and Greek set *him* free from the bondage of superstition? How could he ever learn the Gospel of redemption by the blood of Christ? How could he know that God had spoken, not through the warped and contradictory claims of the Church, but plainly through the Scriptures? There was only one answer. John Ploughman must read the Scriptures for himself, in plain ploughman's English.

Tyndale dropped his gaze to the manor nestling below him on the side of the hill. That was England also. That was so-called Christian Europe. The lord of the manor ruled John Ploughman through a line of descending officials: the steward, the bailiff, the reeve (he knew everyone's business in the village), the hayward and the beadle (or village constable). John Ploughman was at the beck and call of the lord of the manor and he worked many days and weeks in the year for the lord with no payment other than a free meal. The land was the lord's, or if not his, the Church's and the peasant farmer did not even own himself. It was not uncommon for a lord to send a family, or just part of a family, to live in another village if it suited his convenience. Even now the common villager could only marry his sweetheart if the lord of the manor gave permission.

Then, above the manor stood the small square towered church, made of stone and built to last. That also was England and Europe. Even lords and kings were subject to the Church. This vast financial house with the pope as chairman held Europe in a vice-like grip. Everyone lived in fear of the Church and the meanest and most retrograde cleric found protection under its wing, providing he did not expose its weaknesses. The priest was the Church and the Church was the pope and the pope was as nearly God as made no difference. And this is not an extravagant claim, for in his mocking play against Julius II even Erasmus made the pope say, before Peter at the gates of heaven, "He who is in God's place on earth is quasi – God himself". Yet it was never Tyndale's purpose to pull down the Church, but only to establish the Word of God above it.

Even the very spot on which Tyndale sat, gazing down sadly upon the ploughmen, the manor and the church, was a fitting place for the wrestling of his mind. Here on this very hill the Roman legionaries had built a well fortified camp; here the Saxons had entrenched themselves before going out to the battle of Dyrham in 577. And it was here that Edward IV, and his brother Richard (later King Richard III) rested their army before moving off through the early morning darkness of 3rd May, 1470 to the battle of Tewkesbury where the army of Margaret of Anjou was crushed and her son killed. The sons of Sir John Walsh ran and played in the dips and hollows of the old camp, unaware of the cruel battles that lay behind its history, or the fierce struggle that raged in the heart and mind of their tutor.

BRISTOL PREACHING

When Tyndale was not teaching the two boys, climbing Camp Hill, walking in the garden, sitting quietly in the large stone-walled bowling green or by the small lake beyond, he was to be found either engrossed in his books or tramping the fifteen miles to Bristol. The more he studied, the more the Word of God fired his soul to tell others of the liberty that the true Gospel gives. Sir Thomas More was mistaken when he implied that Tyndale had been in "divers places in England" for, apart from his university life, it is doubtful that he had moved far from his home area in Gloucestershire by this time; but the great Lord Chancellor was certainly correct in his admission that the young tutor-priest, "did great good with preaching".

Bristol was a city of six thousand inhabitants, which was twice as many as Gloucester could claim. It ranked with the four other big cities in England, London, York, Coventry and Norwich, each of which could boast something in excess of one thousand homes within its walls. The weary priest approached the large turretted walls, entered the massive gateway and threaded his way down the narrow twisting streets to St. Austin's Green (now College Green). The large wood-framed houses with their overhanging storeys jostled in motley array under the protection of the castle and its lofty and magnificent keep, built upon the high ridge in the centre of the town. Bristol was established in an oval valley crossed by the River Avon on its journey through Bath to the Bristol Channel; to the east and north the town was bounded by the River Frome. The Avon was large and deep and the six main thoroughfares, which were in reality little more than grubby lanes (though some had been newly paved when the High Cross was painted and gilded in 1490) all led to the quay in the centre of the town. Bristol was busy with trade, and wool was its fast-growing merchandise; and since there were three times as many sheep as there were people in England, this was hardly surprising. Thomas Blanket, a citizen of Bristol, set up his large looms there in 1340.

William Tyndale walked down to the shambles where merchants stored their wares for import and export; he passed along King's Street, where the cooks and traders lived in their toy-town houses by the old market place on the east side of the choir of the church of the Friar-preachers. Everywhere there were abbeys, monasteries and chantries (chapels built by the wealthy in which nothing was sung or chanted but masses for their departed souls). Religious houses of one sort or another abounded and their number

was only exceeded by the inns and hostelries. William could
walk down How Street which began at the end of the wall
of the Carmelites' garden and find himself confronted by the
large image of Our Lady placed within an ornate tabernacle.
The town was remarkable for the number of its religious
festivals and if William had tramped into Bristol at Whitsun
he would have been disgusted to see the Guild of Weavers
and Cordwainers (shoemakers) in procession to the Chapel
of St. Anne in the Wood, near Brislington, to place two
enormous candles (some said eighty feet high!) before the
altar. Each candle cost five pounds, which was no small
sum when the mayor was paid only twenty pounds a year.
On 6th December Tyndale could have watched the farce
of the boy bishop installed with full regalia and listened
while the child actually delivered a sermon at St. Nicholas'
Church before the mayor and council. What a religion was
this! But if he preferred, there were always the amusements
of bear-baiting or bull-baiting, two of the town's favourite
sports. In fact bull-baiting had its serious side, for the dogs
tearing at the animals' flesh was supposed to improve the
flavour of the meat!

Bristol was a city of growing wealth; so much so that when
Henry IV visited the city he marked his appreciation for
hospitality received by levying a fine of one pound upon all
citizens worth twenty pounds a year because their wives
were so richly clothed. It was the town from which John
Cabot sailed in 1497 to discover Newfoundland; and in the
very year that Tyndale was preaching here, Bristol was
leading the nation in the manufacture of soap, to be sold in
London at one penny a pound.

Tyndale knew the town and its people well, especially
the preaching-friars. They listened to this serious priest from
Little Sodbury as he stood on St. Austin's green and expounded from Erasmus's New Testament. Here was no
railing and invective; it was a mark of Tyndale's life that he
won respect from even his bitterest opponents. His message
was plain, Scriptural, but hardly the way to earn money in
the sixteenth century. "If thou repent and believe the
promises, then God's truth justifieth thee; that is, forgiveth

thee thy sins, and sealeth thee with His Holy Spirit, and maketh thee heir of everlasting life through Christ's deservings. Now if thou have true faith so seest thou the exceeding and infinite love and mercy which God hath showed thee freely in Christ." Speaking of merits and looking directly at the Augustinian friars around him Tyndale could preach, again as he later wrote, "God hath promised Christ's merits unto all that repent; so that whosoever repenteth, is immediately heir of all Christ's merits, and beloved of God as Christ is. How then came this foul monster (the pope) to be lord over Christ's merits, so that he hath power to sell that which God giveth freely? O dreamers! yea O devils, and O venomous scorpions, what poison have ye in your tails! O pestilent leaven, that so turneth the sweet bread of Christ's doctrine into the bitterness of gall! The friars run in the same spirit, and teach, saying, 'Do good deeds, and redeem the pains that abide you in purgatory . . .' ".

The language sounds hard to the modern ear, but it was restrained for the sixteenth century. Nevertheless the friars were furious at such teaching. Where would their gain be if the people really believed that salvation was a free gift from God? The whole Church would collapse. When Tyndale finished preaching and set out on his long journey home the friars ran to the alehouses, "which is their preaching place" as Tyndale contemptuously commented, and plotted and schemed to silence this young upstart from the universities. And it was not long before the opposition of the friars began to bite.

Periodically the bishop's chancellor would visit the diocese and hold court to deal with matters of Church concern. On one such occasion Tyndale was warned to be sure he was present. The note was ominous and the tutor later recorded how earnestly he prayed, as he walked the lanes to the appointed place, that God would give him strength to stand faithfully in his hour of trial. And he could be in no doubt as to what might be the conclusion of such a trial. Just two or three years earlier news had filtered into the West Country that on 4th April, 1519 a woman and six working men, three of them shoemakers, had been

burned in the Little Park at Coventry for no other crime
than teaching their children the Lord's Prayer, the Ten
Commandments, and the Apostles' Creed *in English*!

When Tyndale arrived at the place of examination he
was arraigned before John Bell, Chancellor and Archdeacon,
and accused of being "an heretic in sophistry, an heretic in
logic, an heretic in his divinity . . ." and so the charges
continued. In fact the drunken friars had embellished his
preaching and invented doctrines Tyndale certainly did not
hold, but they had little need to, for the plain facts of his
views were decidedly against the teaching of the Church of
Rome. He was warned that his patron (Sir John Walsh)
should not be relied upon to protect him from the wrath of
the Church; Tyndale was well aware of this. He was warned
also that if he continued such preaching there were other
measures the Church could take; Tyndale was aware of
this also. When allowed to reply the young reformer answered, "I am content that you bring me where you will into
any country within England, giving me ten pounds a year to
live with, so you bind me to nothing, but to teach children
and preach", which was effectively saying, "Providing I can
go on doing what I am doing, I do not care where I do it".
There seemed no answer to this and the Chancellor, without
extracting any promises of him, let Tyndale return to Little
Sodbury Manor.

AN OLD DOCTOR

For the present, Tyndale had escaped, but the wolves, once
baying, would close on their prey to the kill. About this time
William visited an old clergyman living not far off who was
known to be sympathetic to the views Tyndale had been
expressing. Tyndale felt alone. Many of his old companions
at the universities had already recanted under pressure and
others were fugitives in the country; the kindly sympathy of
Sir John and his wife was hardly the same as a kindred
heart that beat with the same fire of the Gospel. The small
band of those who had been influenced by his preaching
were a great encouragement to him but they were too young
in their faith to counsel the preacher of St. Austin's Green.

He longed for an *evangelical* friend – a word that even
Erasmus and More were beginning to use to refer to the
Gospel men. In 1519 Erasmus wrote to a young Flemish
cardinal and, contrasting the teaching of Luther with the
state of theology in the Church of Rome complained,
"While all the time no word is heard of evangelical doctrine
in the schools of theology". Eleven years later Thomas
More arrested Thomas Hilton, a reformer who was burnt
at Maidstone in March 1530, and claimed to have found in
his possession letters "written from evangelical brethren
here unto the evangelical heretics beyond the sea". The
word *evangelical* was synonymous with the Gospel of the
Reformation.

The old doctor to whom Tyndale now went had once
been archchancellor to a bishop and was decidedly evangelical and a long-standing acquaintance of Tyndale.
Seated in the old man's study, the young priest could un-
burden his mind. He spoke of his hopes and his fears; he
sought wise counsel that he might not throw himself away
foolishly before he had accomplished anything. But above
all he wanted to test his discoveries from Scripture to be
sure that he had rightly understood the Word of God. The
discussion was useful, but the old doctor was a cautious man.
"Do you not know," he concluded, "that the pope is the
very antichrist, which the Scripture speaketh of? But beware
what ye say, for if ye shall be perceived to be of that opinion,
it will cost you your life. I have been an officer of his, but I
have given it up, and defy him and all his works." As
Tyndale walked home his mind was decided. Cautious he
might need to be, but one thing was certain; he would never
trim his views to save his life.

"I DEFY THE POPE"

Those parting words of the old man rung in his ears. They
were easily said, but to live by them meant defiance of every
ruler in Europe.

Sir John and Lady Walsh were known for their hospitality,
and few days passed without travelling friars or higher
Church dignitaries being invited to the large oak table in

the Great Hall. The conversation almost invariably turned
to the great issues of the day. In the European arena 1523
was an eventful year. At the "Field of the Cloth of Gold"
three years earlier the king had signed a perpetual treaty
with Francis of France just four days after he had signed a
similar treaty with Charles V of the Holy Roman Empire;
within twelve months Henry had ratified his permanent
alliance and friendship with Charles whilst he busily
equipped his army and navy to invade France. At home, the
execution of the powerful Duke of Buckingham in 1521 had
sent a cold shiver around the necks of all the noble lords and
encouraged them to contribute the three hundred and fifty
thousand pounds "voluntary" war loan assessed by Wolsey.
Everyone was talking of the new invasion of France planned
by the king, an invasion led by the Earl of Suffolk which, in
the event, achieved nothing but a disreputable trail of
wanton destruction from Calais to within forty miles of
Paris. But still the king was short of money and by April
1523 Parliament was recalled and strangely maintained "a
marvellous obstinate silence" as Wolsey remarked, when
asked for a further eight hundred thousand pounds. This
"Amicable Loan" was bitterly resented in every manor
house. Wolsey's policies and Henry's treasury were bankrupt.
There was much to talk about in the manorial halls this
year. The pope had signed a peace with Francis against
Charles; the Vatican was now standing on its head, but it
was Henry who felt giddy, for the king, strutting around
with his newly acquired title of "Defender of the Faith", had
thought himself on the pope's side when he treated with
Charles against Francis! Charles saved the day by an
unexpected victory over France, actually capturing the
French king. But then Henry was in trouble for not helping
Charles, who was also short of money, faced with a Turkish
advance up the Danube and a peasants' revolt in Germany.
The permanent alliance and friendship of twelve months
ago was looking a little sick. Amidst all these troubles Pope
Adrian VI found it easier to opt out of the European scene.
He died in 1522. The incompetent Clement VII had just
been elected and speculative rumours flew around the courts

The Great Hall at Little Sodbury Manor

and manor houses regarding his politics. Poor Queen Catherine, who had not conceived for four years, was steadily slipping from favour, and court gossip elaborated the stories of Anne Boleyn. In 1523 there was no shortage of table-talk and the king's affairs, of one sort or another, formed the basis of most of it. The large table in every manor house was the place where court and state gossip was passed on and the problems of the world were instantly solved. In this Little Sodbury was little different from the rest of England.

But at Little Sodbury the serious tutor added a new dimension to the conversation. His very presence was at once resented by the great abbots, deans and archdeacons who sat at the table. Tyndale was a mere priest and tutor, and they felt almost insulted that he was allowed to remain at the table. But Sir John had confidence in his tutor and clearly loved to listen to a debate; doubtless it gave him considerable secret enjoyment, not to mention pride, when his young priest silenced his attackers by his power of reasoning, his superior learning and his constant use of Scripture. The conversation inevitably steered to Erasmus and Luther, and the great dignitaries became more than annoyed with a young Oxford graduate who insisted upon arguing against them from a Latin Vulgate which they rarely opened and a Greek New Testament which they were quite unable to read. These mighty contestants took advantage of the occasional absence of Tyndale, probably on his preaching days at Bristol, to disquiet the minds of Sir John and Lady Walsh. On one occasion Tyndale was sent for as soon as he arrived home and his master put to him some of the objections raised at a banquet to which they had been invited that day. William answered from the Scriptures and proved the opinions of the great men to be false. Silence followed. It was clear that Sir John and his wife held Tyndale in the highest regard and were greatly influenced by his life and views. Lady Walsh could think of no way to counter him except by an earthly logic. "Look," she remarked, "there were three doctors of divinity here, one can spend £200 a year, another £100 and the third £300. Surely

we should accept the word of men of such influence and
wealth before that of a humble priest." Tyndale, who
probably earned less than £10 a year plus his keep, had no
answer. If truth was to be judged by such a measure then
there *was* no answer.

It was shortly after this that Tyndale translated Erasmus'
little book the *Manual of the Christian Soldier* and he noticed
that after Sir John and his wife had read this, fewer and
fewer dignitaries were invited to the table. Tyndale's mind
was now decided, he knew what God had called him to do.
He could stay quietly here at the manor and while away his
days in speculation, but that must be for another man.
Tyndale was of a different fibre. Outside, his countrymen
were living and dying in ignorance. No-one cared to give
the ploughman the Truth; no-one cared for his soul. At
last he burst out with his resolve and carried it through,
until his final gasp was choked by the strangler's noose.

A learned man had been debating some point over the
table, and finding he could not get the better of this troublesome Scripture-quoting priest he rose in a rage and stormed,
"We were better be without God's law than the pope's".
That, thought Tyndale, aptly summarised the prevailing
view in the Church of Rome. He broke the pregnant silence
that followed: "I defy the pope and all his laws; if God
spare my life, ere many years I will cause a boy that driveth
a plough shall know more of the Scripture than thou dost".
Doubtless that meal ended in hasty embarrassment!

It was now clear that Tyndale could no longer stay at the
manor. He was far too dangerous. His words were fire. In
fact he had only echoed what Erasmus had penned in his
Greek New Testament in 1516: "I vehemently dissent from
those who are unwilling that the sacred Scriptures, translated into the vulgar (common) tongue, should be read by
private persons . . . I wish that the husbandman may sing
parts of them at his plough, that the weaver may warble
them at his shuttle, that the traveller may with their nar-
ratives beguile the weariness of the way." And those words
circulated with the blessing of the pope. But what popes
said, and what popes meant, were rarely the same thing.

Erasmus was careful not to make the mistake of carrying out his fine words by translating into a "vulgar tongue". He remained the scholar of theory. Tyndale was the scholar of action.

In fact Tyndale's decision was not necessarily unlawful. After Wycliffe and his Lollards an act was passed prohibiting any man from translating the Scriptures without the authority of a bishop. In theory at least, Tyndale required only an episcopal patron. Bishop Tunstall of London was a fine scholar, by reputation liberal in his approach to the new learning, and highly commended by Erasmus. In his simplicity Tyndale reasoned that the opposition of the country clerics was largely because of their gross ignorance; he had only to present himself and his credentials to a man of learning and he could continue his work without further hindrance. His only purpose was to settle in London and translate the New Testament to enable the common man to read it for himself.

Accordingly, Tyndale translated a little speech of Isocrates to demonstrate his ability with Greek, collected a letter of introduction from Sir John Walsh to Sir Henry Guildford, the Controller of the king's Household, packed his few belongings, bade farewell to his master and Lady Walsh and their two boys and, in July 1523, set out for London.

CHAPTER 4

FROM LONDON TO LUTHER
1523-1525

The great city of London was, in fact, very small. It was little larger than Bristol, and yet it was the heart of the nation and the centre for everything that mattered. If the young priest entered the city from the south, he must cross by the old London Bridge. Completed in 1209 this ugly work of stone replaced the original bridge of timber that had burnt down a century before, and provided the only bridge across the Thames into London. The nineteen irregular arches fought bravely to stop the whole structure from toppling into the river. Tyndale threaded his way down the narrow and dark passage at the centre of the bridge. On either side of him houses hung crazily over the water and were only prevented from falling by massive timber beams tying both sides together. The water rushed between the arches and the watermen shouted and bawled at each other. Most of the bridge houses were occupied by the pin and needle makers.

To the wide-eyed priest approaching the city for the first time in the summer of 1523 everything was fascinating. The whole city was guarded, like all medieval cities, by a high and broad wall broken here and there by turrets and large double gates: at Aldgate, Bishopsgate, Cripplegate, Aldergate, Newgate, Ludgate and most probably Bridgegate. On the east, guarding the approach from the sea, was the grim fortress of the Tower. Tyndale noticed also that all the principal streets led into the great market-place, the Cheap, with the homes of the great merchants and traders cluttered

63

The Thames Embankment and part of Old London Bridge about the time of Tyndale

around it, each with its own small garden. Finally there were the religious houses. They were everywhere, just like Bristol. There were homes for the Black Friars, the Grey Friars, the Augustinian Friars, the White Friars, the Crutched (crossed) Friars, the Carthusians, the Cistercians, and priories and nunneries in profusion. The monks at Westminster Abbey outside the city wall cultivated their produce in the Convent Garden and, beyond the city wall to the north, fields and meadowland stretched out towards the deep forests and woods. St. Giles, Clerkenwell, and Barbican were little more than hamlets. Spitel Fields was a vast expanse of open common land. In the Moor Fields to the north of the city young London regularly practised archery at the Artillery Butts, a serious sport that made the English archer such a formidable foe. The English longbow had already won the battles of Crécy, Poitiers, and Agincourt; at Crécy the seven thousand archers did not even allow the splendid French knights to come close enough to fight, and at Agincourt they killed virtually all the horses and left the brave knights encased in their steel on the mud and as helpless as beetles on their backs. As a result, English law demanded that every young man should become, and remain, a proficient bowman, a law which lasted into the early seventeenth century. Just inside the city wall was Grub Street where the grobes or feathers were added to the arrows. Bread Street, Ironmonger Lane, Wood Street, Milk Street, and Poultry Street, all told their own story; even Friday Street, hard by St. Pauls, was so named because it was devoted to the sale of fish for fastdays.

Henry VIII had taken great care to clean up his city and his first act for the paving and the improvement of London described the streets as "very foul and full of pits and sloughs, very perilous and noyous, as well for all the king's subjects on horseback as well as on foot and with carriages". The Hospital of St. Mary of Bethlehem, or Bedlam as it was known for short, was here in the time of Tyndale and cared even then for the insane; a number of other hospitals, including one for lepers and another "for leprous maidens", were scattered about the city.

But if the city was old, something new was happening when William Tyndale arrived in 1523. Cardinal Wolsey had called Parliament in April and demanded money for the new war. Eight hundred thousand pounds would be raised somehow and Wolsey became the most hated man in England. The merchants and traders seethed with anger. His Excellence might call it "An Amicable Loan" if he wished, but no Englishman gave one-sixth of his income to the state amicably. And the whole nation seethed with London. Rumours and reminders of the rebellions of Wat Tyler and Jack Cade flew around the city, and the officers at the Tower Gate kept a wary eye in the direction of troublesome Kent. The king finally decided upon free gifts instead. Wolsey would, of course, introduce the royal change-of-direction, and ensure that the free gifts amounted to not less than was expected of the Amicable Loan. Parliament was dissolved in August.

Tyndale could hardly have chosen a worse time to arrive in London with his dangerous request. At last the commons was asserting itself; Parliament had told Wolsey, and even His Royal Highness, that they could look elsewhere for their money. The bishops felt threatened and reacted as only bishops can – they said, "Not yet" to everything.

Tyndale presented his letters to Sir Harry Guildford, who communicated with Bishop Tunstall and, receiving a not unfavourable response, suggested that if Tyndale would care to write to the bishop's secretary he might gain an interview. The eager reformer took his letter in person to the bishop's palace at St. Paul's churchyard and by September he was called for an interview. It was true that Tunstall was a man of some learning, commended by both Erasmus and Thomas More; it was true also that he enjoyed being a patron of scholars. But there was another side to Tunstall, he was not a man of courage and he could be cold and severe. Tyndale called him later "a still Saturn" and "a ducking hypocrite"; and this was not written in spite, for by then he realised how dangerous it would have been to work in the employ of the bishop. With the unsteady political situation, the rush of Lutheran books into the country, and the fact that Tunstall had only just settled into his comfortable episcopal office, it was hardly a wise move for him to consider employing a zealous Bible translator. The bishop stiffly informed Tyndale that he already had more in his employ than he could adequately support but that he was sure the scholarly priest would find service somewhere in the city.

Tyndale was cast down, but not destroyed. He had tried to translate the New Testament legally and had been refused. But the man behind the plough would have the Scriptures in a plain language – somehow. Years later in 1540 when the Great Bible was issued, bearing most of the work of Tyndale between its pages, Tunstall's name appeared on the title page, authorising it! There are always fearful and accommodating men who revel in the liberty gained by the blood of others.

THE HOME OF MONMOUTH

Whilst Tyndale was waiting for his interview with the bishop, he preached on a few occasions at the Church of St. Dunstan-in-the-West, in Fleet Street. A wealthy cloth merchant by the name of Humphrey Monmouth had recently become "a Scripture man" and as soon as he heard gossip of the preaching at St. Dunstan's, he crossed the three miles from his home and listened to the Gospel from this unknown priest. After a few Sundays he met Tyndale, and, learning that he hoped to be taken into the household of the bishop of London shortly, became closely acquainted with him. It was a friendship that was to benefit Tyndale greatly at the expense of the merchant. Four and a half years later Monmouth was arrested and thrown into the Tower for having once aided the renowned arch-heretic. However, ignorant of his future, Humphrey Monmouth took the rejected priest into his home for six months. Here, according to the merchant in his letter to Thomas More pleading for his liberty, Tyndale "lived like a good priest. . . . He studied most part of the day and of the night at his book, and he would eat but sodden (boiled) meat by his good will, no drink but small single beer. I never saw him wear linen

about him in the space he was with me". Tyndale's simple
food, his cheap, woollen garments, and his serious application to his studies impressed Monmouth as greatly as they
had Sir John Walsh. Monmouth was careful not to reveal
to Thomas More, the Lord Chancellor in succession to
Wolsey, what he must surely have known, that those six
months of unremitting application "at his book" saw
Tyndale commencing his great work of translating the Bible
into English. The merchant admitted that on just one
occasion he had sent a little money to Tyndale when he was
on the continent, by Hans Collenbeke "a merchant of the
Steelyard". That was a dangerous slip.

The Steelyard was situated to the west of London Bridge
and it became the landing point for much of London's
merchandise, in particular wheat, rye and other grains,
cables, masts, tar, flax, hemp, linen and wax. Steel was just
one among many commodities. The trade was virtually
under the control of the Germans who had been there from
as far back as the year 979 and had formed themselves into
a tight community. They were masters in the art of commerce
and were not expelled until 1597 when Queen Elizabeth
thought she could manage without their assistance. The
name of the place in fact had nothing to do with steel but
was derived from the old German *Stapel-hoff*, a general house
of trade (equivalent to the modern *lagerhaus*, or warehouse).
Many favours were granted the German merchants and in
return they undertook to keep the Bishopsgate in good
repair. They were almost all friends of reform and when
Tyndale came to London, Lutheran books were already
arriving in their hundreds at the Steelyard along with the
flax, hemp and linen. Hans Collenbeke was clearly not an
Englishman and these men from the Low Countries were
dangerous friends for Monmouth to have coming to his
home. And so the picture of those six months begins to
emerge.

The home to which Tyndale was now invited may well
have been a three storey building with a seven foot cellar
beneath the whole house. A large entrance hall would most
probably be adjoined by a kitchen which included the

coalhouse, a buttery for wine and beer, a pantry for the bread and a larder for salted meat, fish and vegetables; a cluster of store rooms completed the necessary working part of the home. Servants hustled about busily and kitchen boys turned the heavy crank handles to keep the succulent joints revolving on the spit over the open fire. The home of a wealthy merchant would boast a large parlour, two or three bedrooms, a closet, a business room and even a small chapel. But apart from the parlour, situated to catch as much sun as possible, the whole building was dark and cold; coal fires burnt in the stone hearths but candles, always expensive, were used sparingly and the family and guests economised on heat and light by retiring early to bed. Furniture, even in Monmouth's home, was simple and he might well own the only chair in the house; benches and divans satisfying all other needs. On the large table plates and cups of English or German pewter appeared; spoons were made of horn and dishes of the fashionable green-glazed pottery. No forks appeared anywhere and men still drew a hunting knife from their belt to attack the roast. There were few extras in the sixteenth century merchant home. Servants were cheap but luxury was small. Tyndale required neither. He was happiest with his boiled meat, small beer, and his books. The poor ploughman lived with far less than Humphrey Monmouth and both paled before the glittering splendour of Thomas Wolsey. But for William Tyndale, the greatest necessity for ploughman, merchant and lord chancellor was to own a Bible in the English language.

Humphrey Monmouth was a wealthy man and his large home was constantly invaded by merchants and other businessmen. Monmouth had travelled extensively on the continent and even to Jerusalem; what is more, he had received pardons from the pope. But now he was a "Scripture man", and the talk at his table was very different from that at Little Sodbury. Many of his fellow merchants also loved the Gospel, like Thomas Poyntz, who was a relative of Lady Walsh and who was to play such a vital part in Tyndale's later career. Tyndale listened to the conversation, read the material that came into this Christian home, and pressed on with his translation. John Frith, a brilliant mathematician from King's College, Cambridge, spent many hours in the Monmouth home, talking eagerly of Tyndale's plans.

Perhaps Hans Collenbeke brought a copy of Luther's German New Testament to Tyndale hot from the press in September 1522 but, by whatever means, it is certain that the writings of Luther reached the eager translator. Those men at the Steelyard lived dangerously. Tyndale's great goal was already decided, but now he found in reading Luther that the German reformer's views closely matched his own. Little by little he slipped from Erasmus and held to the position of Luther. The lines of the Reformation were being drawn and Tyndale was quick to see this. Luther did not mould his thinking, he merely confirmed the position Tyndale was already taking.

THE MARKS OF REFORMATION

The great difference between Erasmus and men like Tyndale and Luther was that whereas Erasmus and his fellow reformers within the Church of Rome saw all the abuses and longed for them to be set right, the evangelical Protestant reformers alone went to the *cause* of the evil practices. Tyndale and Luther knew that the cause of the corrupt state of the Church was its corrupt doctrine, and until the doctrine of the Church was corrected, the abuses would continue. On this turned the whole issue of the Reformation. The evangelical reformers were forced out of the Church of Rome, not because they could not accept the corrupt practices, but because they early discovered that the corrupt doctrines could never be changed. This is why they succeeded where the others failed. Morton, Erasmus, More, Colet, Warham and a host of others, all stayed in the Church because for them the doctrine was pure. History reveals that they achieved absolutely nothing in terms of vital reformation. All the world knew, and still knows, how corrupt was the Church in the Middle Ages and how desperate was the need for reform, but it needed men like Tyndale and Luther to tell *why* it was so. They were men of experience, who had a heart relationship with Christ, but they were also more than this. We cannot deny that both Colet and Erasmus were men committed to Jesus Christ but they lacked at one crucial point.

The mark of all the evangelical reformers was that they were men totally committed to the authority of Scripture. It was their final test and source of all doctrine and it towered above princes, prelates and popes. In 1528 Tyndale wrote in his *Parable of the Wicked Mammon*, "Believe not every spirit suddenly, but judge them by the Word of God, which is the trial of all doctrine; and lasteth for ever". *Sola Scriptura*, Scripture alone, was the watchword of the reformers. From this followed the doctrine of justification by faith in the merits of Christ alone. By a papal bull of 1343, *Unigenitus* (the latin *bulla* referred to the pope's lead *seal*), Clement VI asserted that Mary and the saints have been adding to the merits of Christ, and that this great reservoir of merit in heaven has been given to the Church to dispense to the faithful – at a price. The reformers rightly saw that such teaching found no support in Scripture and it savagely attacked the glory of the redemption gained by Christ on the cross. With such teaching the Church was bound to be corrupt; it could be nothing else. But how could the eyes of the common people be opened unless they could read the Scriptures for themselves? Thus the two fundamental doctrines of men like Tyndale and Luther – the absolute authority of Scripture, and salvation by faith in the death of Christ alone, led to an inevitable conclusion: the Scriptures must be translated. Lesser men might flinch from taking up the task in defiance of the pope and his councils. Erasmus admitted his own weakness in a letter to Richard Pace: "I follow the pope and the Emperor when they decide well, because it is pious to do so, I bear their bad decision, because it is safe to do so". Such men could never change Rome, even if they wanted to. Tyndale was a different kind of man.

Tyndale came quickly and sadly to the conclusion that there was nowhere in England he could safely translate the Scriptures, and, when translated, nowhere to print them.

There was only one course open to him. Accordingly, sometime in 1524 Tyndale broke the law of England and slipped
away to the continent without the king's consent.

LUTHER AND HIS CITY

In a copy of the registers of the University of Wittenberg a
strange name appears under the date 27th May, 1524,
Guillelmus Daltici ex Anglia – William Daltici from England.
The date and circumstances fit exactly. The reformer, to
conceal his identity, reversed the two syllables of his name
Dal-tin and a later copyist merely confused the *n* for *ci*.
There was nothing unusual about such a concealment;
Robert Barnes entered himself as Antonius Anglus, in 1533,
though Luther's companion, Melanchthon, revealed all by
scribbling Barnes' proper name in the margin! Tyndale
had begun his desperate game of exile and hide-and-seek
with the royal agents; a game that was to last until his
arrest eleven years later.

The Elbe River wound its way through the northern
lowlands of Germany and turned sharply to the west in
Saxony. At this bend Wittenberg, or the city of the White
Mountain, grew up. Wittenberg was in the land of the
Elector of Saxony, one of six electors who chose the Emperor
and enabled him to rule or misrule. The Elector of Saxony
was Frederick the Wise and this fair-minded, liberal governor
was well named. Frederick began a massive building pro-
gramme to improve the town and this was virtually complete
by the time Tyndale arrived. He rebuilt the castle and
Castle Church, added three public baths to the town and in
1502 established the university which, unknown to him,
was to become indelibly imprinted in the history of Europe.
It was here, around the year 1514, in a little turret room on
the second floor of a curiously shaped building that Martin
Luther discovered in scripture the doctrine of justification
by faith.

Luther was born on 10th November, 1483. He came from
a poor, hardworking copper-mining family, and his father,
by thrift and industry, improved himself sufficiently to own
and rent mines. Luther graduated from the University of

Erfurt in 1505, gained his master's degree and read law. Without warning, on 15th July, 1505, he entered the "Black Cloisters", an Augustinian order of hermits. By 1512 his brilliant mind had earned him a doctorate but his soul was in torment. Luther had been assured that "Upon entrance into the order a monk would be purified like a child who had just received his baptism". But he did not feel this purifying, and being assured that self affliction was the path to holiness, the earnest monk beat himself to wash away his sin. "I myself was a monk for twenty years and so plagued myself with prayers, fastings, wakings, and freezings that I almost died of cold. . . . What else did I seek through this but God? . . . Sometimes I would lock myself up for two or three entire days at a time with neither food nor drink, until I had completed my breviary. My head became so heavy that I could not close my eyes for five nights. . . . I was so imprisoned in this practice that the Lord had to tear me from this self-torture by violence."

In January 1510 Luther walked eight-hundred miles to Rome and in this city of forty thousand people the monk was bitterly disillusioned and disgusted by almost everything he saw. To make matters worse, the pope was away at a war, and it rained almost without ceasing for the entire month. St. Peter's was only a church on paper when Luther visited the city, but everywhere the sacraments were neglected. When Admiral Philip of Burgundy visited Rome two years before Luther he wrote, "The heathen live more chastely and innocently than these people who now draft the ecclesiastical laws for all Christendom". He added that all they cared for was money and things he did not even dare to mention. Erasmus visited the city about the same time and came away grumbling about the "abominable blasphemies against Christ and his apostles" that he had seen there. Luther rushed around this Mecca of extravagance and vice doing all the penances and pilgrimages of a zealous monk. But he could not push from his mind the thought, "Who knows whether this is true". He saw all the relics imaginable, including the wall behind which the three hundred children slain by Herod at Bethlehem were supposed to be buried, presumably with the exception of the one whose skeleton lay in the Castle Church at Wittenberg.

By 1517 Luther was a professor in the University of Wittenberg with three hundred students at his feet. He began to lecture on Paul's letter to the Romans, from Erasmus's Greek New Testament, with an ever-growing awareness of that great doctrine he had discovered in the little square tower. But 1517 brought Luther face to face with a representative of the corrupt system he was to fight so hard, and this encounter precipitated action in the same way that the ignorant cleric at Little Sodbury had stabbed Tyndale into a decisive resolution.

LUTHER AND INDULGENCES

Indulgences began during the Crusades. All who fought for the pope could purchase a guarantee of pardon if they were slain on the battlefield. By the thirteenth century the Crusades had lost their glamour and a valuable source of Church revenue was threatened. A Jubilee Indulgence was offered, and it was such a success that the time scale was systematically reduced until by 1393 Pope Boniface IX sent agents all over Europe with indulgences. In 1343 Clement VI had demanded three steps as conditional for the effective working of an indulgence: sincere contrition, oral confession and good works to prove the first two; only then could a penitent dip into the treasury of merits built up by Christ and the saints. By 1476 the people purchased a *letter* of indulgence which could cover the dead in purgatory. It is an indictment against the Church of Rome that the earliest printed material surviving today is an indulgence printed in 1454. When Leo required money for St. Peter's and his wars, he sold indulgences to Albert of Mainz who employed, among his agents, John Tetzel. Tetzel peddled his wares close to Wittenberg and people, clamouring for a pardon cheap at the price, conveniently forgot the conditions of Clement VI, and it is certain that Tetzel did not trouble to remind them.

Luther was furious. Many of the townspeople waved their indulgence letters at him when he barred them from mass for their disorderly lives. At mid-day 31st October, 1517 the German doctor nailed his ninety-five theses against indulgences to the door of Wittenberg Cathedral, which was the university notice board. Luther's one mistake was in believing that the actions of Tetzel were carried on without the knowledge of the pope. In fact Leo became alarmed only when the returns for the Saxony estates amounted to a mere one-fifth of that expected. But the ninety-five theses were not the isolated protest of an insignificant Augustinian monk; this was the united revolt of the entire faculty and student body of the university, who presented the Elector of Saxony with a strong letter in defence of Luther's action. In two weeks all Germany knew of his action, and in four weeks all Europe.

But in all this Luther saw himself as a true and loyal son of the Church of Rome; the students and faculty saw themselves the same, and even Frederick the Wise wrote to the pope assuring him that if Luther was a heretic he would have expelled him long ago. However, the pope did not agree and wrote of Luther as "that son of perdition". A year or so later, in 1519, Leo changed his mind and, being persuaded that Luther meant no harm, invited him to Rome, offered to pay his expenses and called him "beloved son". But this was the year Maximillian, the Emperor of Germany, died. The pope was so desperate to have the French king, Francis I, put on the throne of Germany that on 21st June he assured the Elector of Saxony that he would offer a cardinal's hat to *anyone* nominated by Frederick, provided he would help the Holy Father in his political strategy. The picture of Luther in a cardinal's hat is staggering! But the Elector understood Luther better than that.

Luther was summoned to Augsburg, Leipzig and finally, in 1521, to Worms. At Worms Luther argued his case with the eloquent John Eck, in front of Charles V himself. But the whole debate was summed up in Luther's final stand. When, in desperation, his accusers urged him to recant, the reformer fixed his eyes upon the assembled company and replied, "Unless I am convinced by the testimonies of the Holy Scriptures or evident reason (for I believe neither in the pope nor councils alone since it has been established that they have often erred and contradicted themselves), I am bound by the Scriptures adduced by me, and my conscience has been taken captive by the Word of God, and I am neither able nor willing to recant, since it is neither safe nor right to act against conscience. God help me. Amen". The hall was thrown into confusion, the emperor left in disgust and the doctor was barely able to escape with his life. When Frederick the Wise asked Erasmus for his opinion of Luther he received the stark reply: "Luther sinned in two respects, namely, that he attacked the crown of the pope and the bellies of the monks".

But Luther's heroic stand at Worms in 1521 was hardly as important as history has made it; it was really only the show-piece where the great issues were staged in one brief scene. The true battle had taken place at Leipzig during the summer of 1519. It was here, whilst Tetzel lay dying at the Dominican Monastery nearby, that Luther met the powerful debater Johan Maier of Eck in Swabia. John Eck, as he was more familiarly known, spent half an hour trying to prove that the Church required a divinely appointed head. Luther replied to this in a sentence; he did not dispute the point, the real issue was *who* is that head? Eck asserted that Christ had withdrawn from the Church on earth and had placed it under the rule of the popes. Luther found little difficulty in proving from Scripture that Christ was still not only with, but head of His Church. He turned Dr Eck to 1 Corinthians 15: 24-25 where it is plainly stated that Christ must reign until the end of time, when He would deliver the Kingdom to His Father, and to Matthew 28: 20 where our Lord promised to be with His disciples "to the end of the age". Luther could even quote from Augustine and Ambrose to support his view that the proof text of Rome, Matthew 16: 18, referred to Christ Himself as the rock upon which the Church was built, and to no other.

John Eck, the most ruthless and feared debater in all Europe, found his arguments torn apart and the Word of God planted in their room. For six days they debated whether the Church was subject to Christ and His Word or

the pope and his word. Then for two and a half days they
turned to purgatory, indulgences and penance. Eck virtually
admitted all the abuses of which Luther accused the Church.
Two weeks of debate concluded with Luther observing that
John Eck penetrated the Scripture "as profoundly as a water
spider penetrates the water" and with John Eck retaliating
with the comment that Martin Luther set up himself as "a
second Delphic oracle who alone has an understanding of the
Scriptures superior to that of any Father". The skirmish was
over, but the lines had been well and truly drawn for the
battle of the Reformation. Luther had made clear *first*,
that the Word of God must be the sole guide in faith and
doctrine, *second*, that the true Church of Jesus Christ was
the invisible body of all true believers and was not founded
upon St. Peter and *third*, that the papacy was a human
governing body, capable of error and itself to be tested by
Scripture. From this latter point, both Tyndale and Luther
were to arrive, within a year or two, at the conclusion that
the sixteenth century papacy was nothing less than the antichrist.

By now Luther's writing had spread all over Europe and
even the pope reckoned him a major problem to deal with.
When the papal representative had arrived in Worms he
could only obtain a small, unheated room and wrote
despondently to his Holy Father, "Nine-tenths of the people
are shouting 'Luther', and the other tenth shouts, 'Down
with Rome' ". Luther's tract *The Babylonian Captivity of the
Church* led to him receiving a bull of excommunication which
he promptly threw into the fire. On 3rd May, 1521, whilst
Luther was returning from Worms, he was "kidnapped"
and, under the assumed name of "Junker Georg" he lived
for a year as a knight in the castle of Wartburg. Here,
protected from his enemies, he completed his German
translation of the New Testament. Five thousand copies were
sold in two months and during the next fourteen years nearly
a quarter of a million copies passed into the land. Luther
returned to his university in 1522 when extremist groups
burned images, desecrated churches and caused general
disorder. "I will preach it, teach it, write it," he told his

enthusiastic congregation, "but I will constrain no man by force, for faith must come freely, without compulsion." Strange words for the sixteenth century.

Tyndale arrived in Wittenberg at a difficult time. Luther's excommunication was causing a severe decline in student enrolment and less than two hundred registered in 1524 (though it was to climb to more than seven hundred at the height of the reformer's fame). In addition the Peasant Revolt in the German States (precipitated by the Countess of Lupfen ordering the peasants to gather strawberries and snail shells during harvest time!) was blackening the cause of reform.

TYNDALE'S INDEPENDENCE

Tyndale arrived at the old Augustinian monastery and was ushered into Luther's study. Both men appeared physically strong. Luther, who was once little more than skin and bone, was now filling out and his strong shoulders and manly proportions betrayed the rugged mining stock from which he came. Tyndale was younger by around ten years, and though neither man was exceptionally tall, both exhibited the spiritual and mental stature required to shake the world. What the two men talked of, if indeed they met alone, neither of them recorded. Perhaps Luther considered the meeting of relative unimportance in the light of his pressing problems, and Tyndale had already begun to draw a veil of silence and mystery over all his movements. Guillelmus Daltin was aware that he would very soon become a marked man and, unlike the German reformer, he would not be able to shelter under the powerful arm of Frederick the Wise.

Tyndale stayed for no more than nine or ten months at Wittenberg, and by April 1525 he was back in Hamburg writing to England for a little money he had left with Humphrey Monmouth. Evidently Tyndale had gone first to Hamburg when he landed on the continent, but had moved swiftly up the Elbe to Wittenberg. By the end of his stay in the great university city, his New Testament was virtually complete. Then why did he not stay and have his work printed here? We can hardly imagine Luther declining such an urgent request. The temptation must have been very great. Here there was relative security, here there were friends, evangelical men, and above all, here Tyndale could take advantage of the university library and consult the learned Melanchthon and Luther himself, as he saw his translation through the press. Luther refused to allow his own German translation to go through the press before his faculty had helped him carefully revise it, and when he turned to the Old Testament, he freely admitted that he and Melanchthon and Aurogallus might spend three or four days upon a few lines of the book of Job. Philip Melanchthon was a prodigious scholar. By the age of fifteen he had gained his bachelor's degree, and two years later his master's; by the time he arrived in Wittenberg in 1518 he had already published a Greek grammar and was considered by some to be such an accomplished Greek scholar that he ranked second only to Erasmus in all Europe. Yet Tyndale left the strong walls of Wittenberg and threw himself into the arena of a cruel world where his printing and constant revision was accomplished always in the expectation of discovery and arrest, and his library must be easily portable as he moved swiftly from town to town. Why?

One of the most obvious answers to this question is the fact that Cologne on the Rhine, where Tyndale actually began his printing, was much closer to England, and as a centre of trade it provided a natural outlet for his testament to find its way to the homeland. But Hamburg was also a mercantile city and it would prove a simple matter to ship the books down the Elbe from Wittenberg to this sea port. Whereas Cologne was a fiercely Roman Catholic town, Hamburg contained many friends of reform and was considerably influenced by Luther. Besides, why did he not, apart from a short visit in 1525, return to Wittenberg to stay? There must be a deeper reason.

The notes that accompanied Tyndale's first edition of the New Testament show, in places, a remarkable similarity to those found in Luther's German translation. In fact his first known writing, the long introduction to the ill-fated quarto edition of the New Testament begun at Cologne, is very largely a paraphrase of Luther's preface to his own New Testament. Similarly, Tyndale's prologue to the epistle to the Romans, which was published in 1529, is for the most part a translation of Luther's work and in many of his later writings Tyndale freely incorporated work of the German reformer. This has led many to assume that he was a mere copyist of the German reformer and that Luther was responsible for the theology and whole approach of Tyndale. In fact nothing could be further from the truth. Tyndale was a servant of no man, his mind was far too large and independent for this. One of the most pressing reasons why Tyndale left the security of Luther's university was simply that he did not wish to become a Lutheran. Even the translations and traces of Luther in his work reveal Tyndale's strength and independence of character. Where he felt the German reformer had well expressed a particular position, Tyndale saw no need to waste his own words upon it. This was not plundering another's work unjustly, for many of his readers would readily recognise the source, as Sir Thomas More certainly did, and Tyndale openly admitted his love for Luther and ran often to his defence when More attacked him. However, Tyndale often altered what Luther had written, and added his own contribution, if he felt he had some better way of expressing the issue. And, of course, the greater proportion of Tyndale's work both in original writing and in translation, is all his own and reveals his complete independence of mind. He was a slave to no man's thoughts. When Thomas More inaccurately spoke of the confederacy between Luther and him as a thing "well known", Tyndale strongly denied it: "When he (More) saith Tyndale was confederate with Luther, that is not truth." But this was not merely a case of one great scholar refusing to acknowledge his debt to another. In many ways Tyndale possessed an even sharper mind than his German counterpart, and he saved England from some of the dangers into which Lutheranism fell.

Luther never quite broke with the Roman view of transubstantiation in the Mass: that is, the belief that the bread and wine literally and physically become the body and blood of

Christ. He substituted a strange view of consubstantiation that was never fully understood by many of his followers or opponents and led to tragic differences and quarrels. Tyndale early accepted the view that the Lord's Supper was a symbolic memorial and left Luther and the Swiss reformer Zwingli to battle over the subtle meanings of "sacramental union". There were far greater struggles to win. Whilst Robert Barnes in England, Martin Luther in Germany and Huldreich Zwingli in Switzerland were busy attacking each other's position on this issue and bringing discredit to the reformation, it was Tyndale who, as a lone voice, pleaded for an end to the battle. Leave the subject alone, he urged John Frith in prison; let us close our ranks on the great issues of salvation and allow one another a free conscience on matters of secondary importance.

Similarly, Tyndale never countenanced some of the Lutheran scruples over certain books of the Bible. Luther found his doctrines in Paul's letters to Rome and Galatia in particular and ranked the other epistles below these two; James, which always puzzled Luther, was considered "an epistle of straw". Tyndale's independence of Luther at this point is very significant. Luther wrote of the epistle of James, "Though this epistle were refused in the old time, I still praise it and think it to be good, because it setteth up no man's doctrine and pushes God's law hard. But my opinion is, yet without expressing it to anyone's disadvantage, *that it is not written by an apostle. Therefore I cannot place him within the rightful main books*; but I do not want to deny to anyone that he places him as he wishes; as a lot of good verses are in there". Similarly on the Epistle of Jude Luther commented, "Nobody can deny that it is an extract or copy of St Peter's other epistle . . . and contains also verses and stories which are to be found nowhere in Scripture. Although praising it, *it is an unnecessary Epistle to be placed amongst the main books which are laying the foundation of faith*". We must not be too hard in our judgement of Luther; every great man has his weaknesses. But the danger of these ill-conceived doubts is obvious and as a result Lutheranism developed a more critical approach to the Bible leading eventually to the onslaught of the nineteenth century higher critics in Germany. Tyndale saved England from leading the way into such criticism, for he had no such doubts.

Tyndale was well aware of these views of Luther and critically examined them, coming to opposite conclusions. Of the Epistle of James he concluded, "Methinketh it ought of right to be taken for Holy Scripture" and of Jude he claimed, "I see not but that it ought to have the authority of Holy Scripture". Similarly, where Luther cast doubts not only upon the authorship but also upon the authority of the Epistle to the Hebrews, Tyndale allowed the former to be open to question but closed the door firmly against any doubt as to its right to be in the canon of Scripture. In his New Testament the English reformer boldly entitled the book, "Paul to the Hebrews". "Why should it not be authority" he challenged the doctor of Wittenberg, "and taken for Holy Scripture?" Contrary to his German counterpart, Tyndale made no suggestion of treating some New Testament books as more valuable than others.

In his translation work Tyndale showed the same independence of mind. He had no English translation beside him, not even a handwritten copy of Wycliffe's Bible; whereas Luther had no fewer than nineteen German translations to drive off the field. It is certain that Tyndale had Luther's New Testament before him on his desk and in addition he could make use of Jerome's Latin Vulgate, the Bible of the medieval Church. But the latter was in many places inaccurate and nowhere did Tyndale repeat its errors. Apart from these two, Tyndale may have possessed no other text than Erasmus's Greek New Testament which he used with great ability. In all his translation Tyndale reveals a scholarly refusal to be cast into the mould of Luther or Jerome. The same was true of his Old Testament work. When he translated Jonah in 1531, he probably had, besides his Hebrew Bible, the Latin Vulgate, possibly Pagninus's Latin Bible of 1528, Luther's German Bible and the Greek Old Testament (the Septuagint), but again and again he strikes out boldly on his own, a slave to no-one. J. F. Mozley, his chief biographer and one who particularly compared the translation of Jonah concludes, "Throughout he is his own master and, what is more, he usually comes down on the right side". Even in his marginal notes and comments Tyndale takes his own path where he must. It is certainly true that in his notes on the Scriptures Tyndale leant heavily upon the German reformer, but it is very significant that when Luther's interpretation ran counter to his own he held to his own view, and if Luther's mind ran too free with Scripture, such as his fanciful allegory comparing Paul's intercession with Philemon on behalf of Onesimus with Christ's intervention between us and God, Tyndale simply ignored it altogether. As we shall see later, even on the controversial issue of the king's divorce, Tyndale defied friend and foe alike and took up a sensible and Scriptural position. If he did not rank with Luther in the breadth of theological grasp, Tyndale was certainly a most able expositor of the Word of God.

Thus to maintain his independence of mind, Tyndale learnt what he could at Wittenberg, completed his translation and went out to give his own New Testament to the English speaking world. Besides, in that year no other Englishman registered at the university and the quiet priest from the heart of the Gloucestershire countryside was human enough to long for a compatriot with whom he could talk.

CHAPTER 5

A BOOK FOR THE PLOUGHBOY
1525-1527

Tyndale was glad of the hospitality offered to him by the Emmerson family in Hamburg. Perhaps the exile had been recommended to them by one of those Lutheran Steelyard workers, but whatever the introduction, it was a happy relationship, and one that provided some degree of security during uncertain days. Evidently Tyndale hoped to meet a fellow worker at Hamburg; one who would labour with him in the Gospel. But when the unnamed friend failed to arrive, Tyndale, hearing that a certain William Roye had recently come to Wittenberg, shuttled back to Luther's city and returned to Hamburg with Roye.

William Roye was a friar from Greenwich, who had been influenced by the new views, and, being hasty and hot-headed, threw himself into the fray. He proved a troublesome companion and Tyndale freely admitted he could only keep him in check by keeping him short of money, which was not hard since Tyndale had little enough to spare. Three years later the reformer remarked that he was glad to be rid of the man and he "bade him farewell for our two lives, and a day longer".

During the month of August the two men slipped into Cologne, the most populous town in Germany. It was a teeming city of merchants and for many years had been the centre of printing in north-west Germany. Caxton learned the art of printing here between 1471-1472, before he set up his own press close by Westminster Abbey five years later. Books tumbled off the presses and easy access down the

Rhine to the Channel made it a trading centre. In such a large and cosmopolitan town it should not have been hard for the two men to be lost from view, but nothing was to prove easy with a man like Roye around. Although in 1497 the university had obtained a papal privilege extending its censorship to printed books, Peter Quentel, a strong Roman Catholic, was willing to set up his press for the new manuscripts offered him. After all, he was an old man now and had little to lose; besides, most printers would publish anything provided they were paid for it. Each day Tyndale and Roye visited the printing house to check the copy and provide more manuscripts.

Printing was a laborious task in the sixteenth century and the printer invariably pulped his own paper as well. Linen rags were washed, steeped in water, pulped, diluted and poured into a tray with a wire mesh bottom. The water drained off and the sheet of fine pulp that was left was hung out to dry. But the effort was worth while, for the resulting paper was so much cheaper than the more durable calf skin known as vellum. The actual printing required skill, precision and patience. The metal type was placed in a frame on the press and inked by rubbing it with leather balls impregnated with ink. A sheet of paper was placed over the type and the heavy plate of the press screwed down onto it. This was then released, the printed sheet laid aside to dry and a new one inserted. Up to eight pages could be printed on one frame and the sheets were then folded, cut and bound. It was a slow and cumbersome process, but for its day it was revolutionary. The Chinese may have been printing from hand-carved wooden blocks from the ninth century, and making paper from the second, but the first paper mill was not established in England until 1490, and the very first book to come off a European press was a Latin Bible in 1455. Tyndale and Roye watched the sheets laid out to dry; the translator's dream was coming true. John Ploughman almost had his Bible. Almost, but not quite. The essence of success for Tyndale was to act with speed. He had left England less than fifteen months previously and already the press was working. Sooner or later he would be missed

Tyndale translating the Scriptures

in high places, and the king's agents would be alerted.

Discovery

John Cochlaeus was a bitter opponent of the reformers and considered it his life's mission to write against them at every opportunity. He had been forced to flee from both Frankfurt and Mainz when the populace refused to share his extreme views and he settled at Cologne shortly after the arrival of Tyndale and Roye. Cochlaeus was seeking to publish the works of Rupert of Deutz who had been an abbot on the other side of the Rhine four hundred years earlier. He persuaded Peter Quentel to print the material and whilst he was busy around the print shop, editing the manuscripts for the press, he overheard a conversation about an English New Testament. Cochlaeus, according to his own report, gained the friendship of a few workmen and, plying them with wine, learned that soon all England would be Lutheran whether the king or cardinal liked it or not. He discovered also that two learned Englishmen were lurking in the city, and that funds for the printing were liberally provided by the merchants; the three thousand copies ordered had already reached the section K, somewhere in Mark's Gospel. More than satisfied with his information, Cochlaeus went to a senator of Cologne, Hermann Rinck, whom he knew to be a friend of Henry VIII, and revealed the whole plot. When Tyndale and Roye visited the press the following day, they little realised that the inquisitive stranger discussing some pretended business was the senator's personal investigator. The Senate at once ordered the seizure of the paper and type, and the arrest of the two Englishmen.

News somehow leaked through to the two reformers and, seizing armfuls of printed sheets, they slipped away by night up the Rhine to Worms. But the news was out. Cochlaeus may have been robbed of his prey but he wasted no time in writing to the king and a strict watch was set on all the ports. Unfortunately for Cochlaeus he was robbed of his reward as well, and years later he was still complaining that he received nothing for such a valuable service to His Majesty. Bitterly disappointed though Tyndale must have

been, the translator never once referred to this despicable
man, and it is certain he knew his identity for Roye took
his revenge in print a year or two later. The king shortly
received a letter from Edward Lee his newly appointed
ambassador to Spain who, whilst making his way to his new
court, had also heard of this daring Englishman. He urged his
royal master to take speedy remedial action against this
translation of the New Testament into English which would
soon be on its way into England and added, "I need not to
advertise your grace what infection and danger may ensue
hereby, if it be not withstanded". Just in case his sovereign
had forgotten, Edward Lee presumed to remind the king
that "All our forefathers, governors of the Church of
England, hath with all diligence forbad and eschewed
publication of English Bibles". And as a final encouragement:
"Now sir, as God hath endued your grace with Christian
courage, to set forth the standard against these Philistines,
and to vanquish them, so I doubt not but that he will assist
your grace to prosecute and perform the same, that is to
undertread them, that they shall not now again lift up their
heads, which they endeavour now by means of English
Bibles".

1526: THE ENGLISH NEW TESTAMENT

Tyndale was not the man to surrender after losing the first
skirmish. He would win the battle at the hazard of his life.
The two men crept furtively into the city of Worms feeling
themselves more than conspicuous with their heavy load of
contraband. This was the city of Luther's heroic stand four
years earlier and the city had since then practically gone
over to the side of the reformer. But whereas Luther entered
Worms in 1521 preceded by the Emperor's herald, protected
by the Elector's authority and accompanied by Saxon
nobles and a crowd of around two thousand who escorted
him to his inn, Tyndale and Roye came to the city with no
human patronage at all, but only a sure faith in the Everlasting God and a firm resolve that His work would be
accomplished. A printer was found, Peter Schoeffer, and the

work proceeded without hindrance. The Cologne sheets were evidently bundled into incomplete books and sent out as they were. They were quarto copies, and the only existing portion ends at Matthew 22. The new edition was to be smaller, printed on octavo and, to speed the six thousand copies through the press, Tyndale deleted the long prologue and two sets of glosses. Assuming that Tyndale arrived in Worms during September 1525 the printing could hardly have been finished before the new year and the first copies must have trickled into England during the spring of 1526.

This was a frightening year on the continent of Europe. Suleiman the Magnificent, the powerful ruler of the Moslem world, swept through Hungary with an army of more than one hundred thousand men; leaving a terrible trail of devastation behind him he sold into slavery one hundred thousand captives. But it was a year of hope for England, for the first printed copies of the English New Testament were smuggled past the vigilance of the royal agents and arrived into the eager hands of student and peasant alike. But God had also been preparing the way in England. The winter of 1525-1526 had been severe for illness; Tunstall, the arch-enemy of the Bible, was out of the country until August and Wolsey and Henry were preoccupied with affairs of state. The disastrous harvest of the previous summer left England in near famine conditions and when Wolsey, in an attempt to conserve the dwindling corn stocks forbade grain to be moved from one county to another, London almost died. The Mayor and Aldermen threatened the Chancellor, "Either the people must die from famine, or else they, with a strong hand, will fetch corn from them that have it". Wolsey pacified them with the false assurance that the King of France had declared his love for England to the extent that if he had only three bushels of wheat in France, he would send two to England. In fact, of course, no grain arrived from France. However this was all part of the plan of a greater Sovereign, for at the very time that grain could not be bought in London for any price, and the capital was ready to exercise its "strong hand", the men from the Steelyard began importing wheat so fast that it became cheap

and plentiful. But with the cargoes of grain another seed
was smuggled in, a seed more precious and more necessary
to England than all the wheat in the world. If the German
Steelyard merchants rescued England from a famine of
corn, they certainly provided also that Bread of Life which
would satisfy the nation's spiritual hunger.

A near perfect copy of this Worms New Testament still
exists. The print is clear and bold and twelve small woodcuts
depict the apostles and the scene at Pentecost. Tyndale did
not break up the chapters into the artificial verse divisions
that we have become accustomed to. The order of books is
that of Luther's Bible. It follows our customary order to
Philemon and then continues: the epistles of Peter, John,
"Paul to the Hebrews", James, Jude and Revelation. An
"Errata" corrected the few printer's errors that Tyndale and
Roye failed to pick up and the whole concluded with a short
epistle "to the Reder". This epistle is a model of brevity and
clarity. The translator began:

"Give diligence dear Reder (I exhorte the) that thou come
with a pure mynde and as the Scripture sayth with a syngle
eye unto the wordes of health and of eternal lyfe: by the
which (if we repent and beleve them) we are borne a newe
created a fresshe and enjoye the frutes off the bloud of
Christ." Tyndale urged his readers to notice the plain and
clear parts of Scripture and to be careful in hard places not
to add anything contrary to that which is plain. Notice also,
he continued, the difference between the law and the Gospel.
"The one axeth (*asks*) and requyreth, the wother perdoneth
and forgeveth." After briefly urging his readers to repent
and believe the Gospel, Tyndale turned his attention to
"them that are learned in Christianity". If his language
offends them he requests pardon, but reminds them that he
had no-one to copy and no-one from the past to help him
with his English (Roye had joined him too late to be of
much help). It was therefore open to future revision: "Count
it as a thynge not havynge his full shape"; and such a
revision the translator promised to undertake as soon as
possible. The work had been done for the edifying of
Christ's body, "which is the congregation of them that

beleve", and the little epistle ends with the simple request "Praye for vs".

During the spring of 1526 the merchant ships that traded between England and the continent began to deliver their precious cargo to the docks and warehouses of London. For the first time in the long history of the nation, a printed English New Testament was available for those who could afford to pay one shilling and eightpence for an unbound copy or a shilling extra for a bound copy. The merchants were careful to conceal the contraband amongst more legitimate items for import and certainly the first copies to arrive reached friendly hands in safety. Although Tyndale's name did not appear on this first edition, there was no difficulty in disposing of the copies and eager hands reached out for the precious book. It was not long before the New Testament had passed through the great cities and the two universities into the possession of even the humblest men and women: apprentices, tailors, founders, saddlers, weavers, bricklayers, servants, fishmongers; wherever a poor man or woman could be found able to read, a few would club together and buy a copy of the Scriptures. The price was relatively cheap, probably not more than half a week's wages for a labourer, and the demand grew. Poor men would offer a load of hay for a New Testament. Alongside the Worms edition came the fragment rescued from Cologne. Tyndale was reluctant to waste what had already been achieved and thus his first attempt, cut off probably at the end of Mark's Gospel, was roughly bound and sent out. Thus we read of a larger book, with glosses, and a smaller one without. The smaller one was in fact the complete New Testament from Worms.

A BOOK TO BURN

However careful the merchants were, it was inevitable that sooner or later a copy would fall among enemies. By the late summer Bishop Tunstall was home again and boiling with rage over the copy in his hand. The bishops met in conclave, but the result of their deliberations hardly required a meeting. The book must be searched out and burnt; strict watch must be maintained at the ports, and government agents were dispatched to check all incoming merchandise. It was made a serious offence to buy, sell or even handle the book. The bishops acted with unaccustomed haste to stamp on the Gospel before it stamped on them. On 24th October Tunstall wrote to his archdeacons complaining of the "holy gospel of God" in the common tongue which was inter- mingled with "certain articles of heretical depravity and pernicious erroneous opinions, pestilent, scandalous, and seductive of simple minds . . . of which translation many books, containing the pestilent and pernicious poison in the vulgar (common) tongue, have been dispersed in great numbers throughout our diocese; which truly, unless it be speedily foreseen will without doubt infect and contaminate the flock committed to us, with the pestilent poison and the deadly disease of heretical depravity". At this point the bishop seems to have exhausted himself of expletives; but such language was calculated to make the most indolent archdeacon wake up and take action! Within thirty days all copies must be called in, upon pain of excommunication and the charge of heresy. The following day the bishop marshalled the London booksellers before him in a private chapel and warned them, in no uncertain terms, of the consequences of handling Lutheran books, whether in Latin or English.

St. Paul's Cross, outside the west door of the great cathed- ral in London, had become a traditional site for important announcements by the Church leaders. It was here that, a few days after his injunction to the archdeacons, Bishop Tunstall preached a strong sermon against Tyndale and his Bible, in which the bishop claimed to have found three thousand errors, although the most searching of modern scholars seem to fall well behind the bishop in such dis- coveries. So eager were the opponents of the New Testament to discredit Tyndale's translation, that Tyndale facetiously remarked that if they found so much as a letter *i* undotted they would lay it bare as a mark of heresy! Tunstall then ceremoniously threw a copy of the New Testament into a blazing fire which had been prepared for the purpose.

Hearing of this action the translator commented in 1527, "In burning the New Testament they did none other thing than I looked for; no more shall they do if they burn me also, if it be God's will it shall so be. Nevertheless, in translating the New Testament I did my duty . . .". By 21st November even Cardinal Campeggio had heard in Rome of the "sacred codex of the Bible, perverted in the vernacular tongue and brought into the realm by perfidious followers of the abominable Lutheran sect". In February of the following year the king stirred himself to declare: "We . . . with the deliberate advice of Thomas Lord Cardinal and other reverend fathers of the spirituality, have determined the said and untrue translations to be burned, with further sharp correction and punishment against the keepers and readers of the same".

But the die was cast; never again would England be without its Bible. Couriers were intercepted, hundreds of copies were burned, people high and low were thrown into prison, even those troublesome merchants in the Steelyard were ordered to swear not to deal with such literature, but still copies poured into the country. Christopher van Endhoven, a printer at Antwerp, had produced a pirate edition by the end of 1526. It was smaller than Tyndale's Worms edition and thus easier to smuggle. By the beginning of November, John Hackett, the English ambassador to the Low Countries, had received letters from Wolsey to deliver to Princess Margaret, regent of the Low Countries, and to the Governor of the English House of Merchants in Antwerp. Endhoven was arrested and, after an infuriating delay for Hackett, his books and presses were destroyed. But it was impossible to recall those books that had already fled across the channel into England. Even St. Andrews and Edinburgh in Scotland were receiving cargoes of the New Testament by the close of 1526. Where a profit is to be made, printers will print and any book so persecuted by the authorities will be sure of a ready market. Hackett found himself commuting between Antwerp and Frankfurt, Barrow, Zeeland and elsewhere seizing books and printers. Too late he discovered that at the April (1527) Book Fair in the great literary centre of Frankfurt "more than two thousand such like English books" were for sale. In rage he stood by the harbour in Zeeland learning that a ship carrying a cargo of Testaments for Scotland had left a day earlier. But Hackett was not always frustrated in his plans, and many hundreds of books and Testaments were destroyed on the Continent.

By May 1527 Archbishop Warham devised a new plan for ridding the world of this pestilent book. He requested his bishops to help share the cost of buying up all the copies available. The prelate must have been a rather naïve financier seriously to believe that sufficient demand would throttle supply! Bishop Nix of Norwich contributed over six pounds to the total of sixty-two pounds nine shillings and fourpence that the archbishop had already so selflessly expended on the project, and complimented his superior upon such "a gracious and blessed deed". Even Tunstall had learnt no better when, two years later, he arranged through a merchant to buy up a large stock of Testaments. By this grand purchase everyone was well satisfied; the bishop had his Testaments to burn, the merchant had his thanks and a reasonable consideration and Tyndale received the money to finance his next edition!

The year following the arrival of the first New Testament, concerted action was taken against those who persisted in reading it. Thomas Bilney, "little Bilney" as he was affectionately known by the reformers, was arrested in November 1527 at Cambridge. Brought to trial in London he recanted and carried his faggot to the pile of burning books in St. Paul's Churchyard, under the pompous eyes of Wolsey who sat in magnificent state. Dr Barnes was next in line for humiliation.

ROBERT BARNES AND HIS FAGGOT

Born near Lyn in Norfolk around 1495, Barnes entered the house of the Austin Friars at Cambridge ten years later. He was a student at Cambridge in 1514 and later went to Louvain to continue his studies in 1517, returning to Cambridge around 1521. He became prior of the Austin friars and after lecturing on the epistles of St. Paul was soon gathering at the White Horse Inn near the Friary with the group of young reformers. Two of the members of this group, Heath and Parker, became archbishops; seven of them became bishops: Gardiner, Fox, Shaxton, Latimer, Cox, Bale and Ridley; and eight of them became martyrs: Bilney, Tyndale, Clark, Frith, Lambert, Barnes, Ridley and Latimer. Thomas Bilney made a great impression upon Barnes, turning him "wholly unto Christ", just as he influenced Hugh Latimer. Barnes preached his first sermon after his conversion, on Christmas Eve 1525, a sermon for which he was immediately dubbed a heretic. In this sermon he declaimed against the superstitious observance of holidays, the pride and pomp of the prelates and the clergy; the rigour and abuses of the ecclesiastical courts; the corruptions and errors of the church; and the persecution of the advocates of religious truth. Twenty-five articles of offensive propositions were presented to the vice-chancellor of the university in accusation against him! In fact his heresy was not so much against the doctrines of the Church but against its practice; he had dared to challenge the lives of the clergy.

When Barnes stood firm the vice-chancellor gave him eight days to reconsider and sent a messenger to inform Wolsey that there was heresy at Cambridge. Wolsey was in the very process of his active campaign against the importing of Lutheran books and Tyndale's New Testament. Barnes was arrested on 5th February. A search was made for Lutheran books but fortunately the word had been already passed around and few were discovered. Barnes's case was heard before Wolsey and he refused to recant. When on the third day of his trial he was presented with a form for recantation he refused to read it. On the promise that the cardinal would be "gracious" to him he read it, subscribed to it, and was absolved by the Bishop of Bath on the condition that he fulfilled penance. Shrove Sunday, 11th February, 1526, was his day of humiliation. With four Steelyard Lutherans he carried a faggot of wood at St. Paul's under the elevated scaffold upon which sat Wolsey and thirty-six abbots, friars and bishops in all their damask satin and purple, against which Barnes had declaimed. They knelt before the bishops and cardinal pleading publicly for forgiveness; baskets, full of offending Lutheran books and New Testaments, were carried outside to be burned. Three times Barnes and the others walked round the fire and on the third time threw the faggot into the flames. They were given final absolution by Fisher and were thus received back into the church.

For the next few months Barnes was placed in the Fleet prison where he had liberty to see his friends while he waited the cardinal's pleasure. He was not allowed to return to Cambridge but was sent to the Austin Friars at London where he was "a free prisoner" for almost two years. Barnes appealed to the Bishop of London but with no success. However it is clear that by September 1526, scarcely six months after his abjuration, Barnes had established a centre for the sale and distribution of Tyndale's New Testament at the house where he was a prisoner.

In 1528 a number of London citizens urged the bishop to release Barnes and in response he was hustled off to Northampton where he was kept under much closer supervision. From here Barnes effected an elaborate method to escape. Claiming that he was going down to the waterside to drown himself, he left a note to encourage those who discovered it to recover his body and an important letter for the cardinal which was tied around his neck. For seven days they dragged the river bottom. Meanwhile Barnes donned a "poor man's apparel", made his way to London, then to Antwerp and finally to Luther's city.

But the case of Dr Barnes was one among many. These were desperate days and the privilege of possessing an English New Testament was accompanied by trials which were taking their toll. This was a serious battle for God's Word and the eternal welfare of the souls of men, altogether unlike Henry and Thomas Wolsey playing soldiers outside the walls of Thérouanne thirteen years earlier. Cardinal Wolsey ordered a rigorous search of London, Oxford and Cambridge. These, he rightly assumed, were the centres to which the New Testament would find its way most speedily.

Just opposite Bow Church in London, down the narrow and dark Honey Lane near Cheapside, stood the Church of All Hallows. The curate, Thomas Garrett, spent much of his time collecting Testaments and other forbidden books from the merchants and travelling the dirty and dangerous roads from the city to the universities. By the beginning of 1528 a search was made for Garrett in London, but he had already left, and when the agents arrived in Oxford they discovered that Garrett had brought three hundred and fifty books to the university in the past few months. Garrett left the town in disguise but he returned and was arrested; he escaped only to be taken once more and imprisoned.

Many young men were arrested at this time and ironically ten of them, like John Frith and Richard Taverner, came from the Cardinal's College. These were the best men at Oxford since Wolsey had personally chosen them, from the cream of the other colleges, to be educated at his new pride and joy. Like everything else Wolsey did his college was to be "the most glorious in the world". At least, unknown to the Lord Chancellor, this description well fitted some of his students. Many of the new prisoners were lodged in the cellars beneath the college, cellars in which salted fish was stored. Three died in the foul conditions, most recanted and Frith, released somewhat unexpectedly, jumped his parole and escaped to the Continent around December 1528.

But many of these men only put off today the inevitable fight of tomorrow. Later, when the New Testament had had time to run in their veins and nerve them for the fire, men like Bilney, Barnes, Garrett and Frith all perished boldly at the stake for their loyalty to the Word of God and the evangelical faith. Many more were little known. Simon Fyshe became a courier for the Antwerp merchant, Richard Herman, and fled twice to the Continent when the chase became too hot; he died, less heroically than others, from the plague in London.

By 15th March, 1527 Tunstall had filled his prisons to overflowing, not merely with young intellectuals from the universities, but with blacksmiths, bakers, weavers and the like. It is true that wealthy merchants, like Humphrey

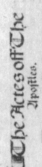

A page from the 1526 New Testament

Monmouth, were incarcerated as well, and even Tyndale's brother John was under suspicion by the authorities, but there is ample evidence that within months of its arrival the English ploughboy was reading the New Testament in his native tongue, or listening to a neighbour reading it to him. Tyndale's resolve was accomplished, but he had much work still to do.

WHAT SORT OF BOOK?

When Tyndale sat down to his translation, he had no-one to guide him, no vast library at his disposal, no friendly scholar to check and criticise his work, no books on the principles of translation and no model from which to copy. He was alone, as he almost always was. The principles upon which he based his work were hammered out in the small attic room at Little Sodbury Manor, not at Wittenberg. By universal agreement, Tyndale succeeded in his great aim; his language and style broke free from the stilted medieval scholastic approach. Tyndale's New Testament was earthy, almost rustic and certainly plain enough for the ploughman. He made the Bible what God had intended it to be: a book for the people.

Tyndale was a master of languages. Buschius, who met Tyndale on the Continent, was slightly in error when he claimed the translator was "so skilled in seven tongues, Hebrew, Greek, Latin, Italian, Spanish, English, French, that whichever he speaks, you would think it his native tongue", for it is certain that Tyndale also mastered German, and was quite capable of understanding the finer points of Luther's writings. How else could he have so accurately disagreed with Luther here and there, or incorporated so much of the German reformer's material into his own work? Tyndale used mainly the Greek Text of Erasmus. Never before had an English translation been made directly from the original Greek. Wycliffe used the Vulgate, an inferior Latin translation. Tyndale also had available Erasmus's own Latin translation, and Luther's *Das Newe Testament Deutzch* which first came off the press in 1522. It is doubtful whether Tyndale ever possessed a copy of Wycliffe's Bible;

they were, of necessity, all old and handwritten and few
copies existed. Tyndale was clearly a good Greek scholar,
equal to Erasmus, Luther and Melanchthon, and there were
probably no better in Europe than these four. He made
mistakes, of course, but many of these he corrected in his
1534 revision. We have already noted that Tyndale frequently exercised his independence and struck out on his
own, parting company from the three versions lying on the
table before him. In 1532, when Tyndale wrote to John
Frith who lay in the Tower of London under the threat of
death, he spoke of his overriding principle in translation: "I
call God to record, against the day we shall appear before
our Lord Jesus, to give a reckoning of our doings, that I
never altered one syllable of God's Word against my conscience, nor would this day, if all that is in the earth, whether
it be pleasure, honour or riches, might be given me". If any
confirmation is required, B. F. Westcott, the nineteenth
century critic who is considered by many to be the greatest
scholar ever to compare the early translations of the Bible,
concludes, "He deals with the text as one who passed a
scholar's judgement upon every fragment of the work,
unbiased by any predecessor". Then why was his translation
so abused?

There is really only one answer to this. The Scriptures in
English would allow every man, even the ploughman, to
test the Church, its doctrines and practice, for himself. And
that would be disastrous. But the Church leaders could
hardly admit this, so other reasons must be found. Warham,
Tunstall and Thomas More accused Tyndale of wilfully
distorting the text to suit his own views. In fact Tyndale
had deliberately dropped certain words in preference for
new ones that avoided the implications of Rome's false
teaching. Early in 1527 a complaint was addressed to
Warham that "by this translation we lose all these Christian
words, *penance, charity, confession, grace, priest, church* . . ." and
this was correct. Tyndale preferred: *repentance, love, acknowledge, favour, senior* (which in 1534 he improved to *elder*) and
congregation. The Church's use of these terms did not agree
with what the Scriptures meant by them and Tyndale's

replacements set the words free from their traditional interpretations. One of the strongest, and legitimate, criticisms of the King James' Authorised Version in 1611 was that it reverted to the use of words like *charity* (which, far from conveying the meaning of the New Testament word "love", referred to the good works of almsgiving to earn merit), *confess* (which had only one interpretation to Rome and that was confession to a priest), *grace* (which was solely administered by the Church), and *Church* (which could only mean Rome and was a denial of the reformers' view of the Church as "the congregation of them that believe"). Small issues now perhaps, but men's lives hung upon them in the sixteenth century. In each case Tyndale, judged merely as a translator, was perfectly correct in his changes. He violated no law of translation, only that of the Church tradition. Many of the criticisms of bias levied at Tyndale are found to hit Erasmus and the Vulgate instead, for on occasions he was borrowing from them! But then, Thomas More was a bosom friend of the great Dutch scholar and Erasmus could therefore never err. More was at least honest enough to admit this.

Tyndale's style was brilliant. It is rich in variety and he refused to be tied to a stilted word for word translation; even though he claimed that the Greek so easily fell into the English that this could in fact be done. For the phrase *it came to pass*, he sometimes inserted *happened, chanced, fortuned,* or *followed*. Even the word *lo* may become *behold, mark, see, look,* or *take heed*.

Sometimes he overplayed this variety and sacrificed accuracy, as for instance in Romans 13: 7, "Give to every man therefore his duty; tribute to whom tribute *belongeth,* custom to whom custom is *due,* fear to whom fear *belongeth*; honour to whom honour *pertaineth*". One Greek word covers them all! Similarly in Matthew 24: 34, "This generation shall not *pass,* till all be fulfilled. Heaven and earth shall *perish,* but my words shall *abide*".

Tyndale sought out words for the ploughman to understand. *Under-Captain* was preferred to *Centurion, excommunicate* to *put out of the synagogue,* and *lay people* to *ignorant men.* He chose phrases that have remained as part of our English heritage:

Matthew 20:12, "Borne the burden and heat of the day";

Luke 12: 19, "Take thine ease, eat, drink and be merry";

Acts 17: 28, "For in him we live, and move and have our being". And many, many passages from this 1526 edition ring familiarly in the ears of those who are acquainted with the King James Authorised Version of 1611;

Colossians 3: 22, "Not with eyeservice, as men pleasers, but in synglenes of herte, fearynge god";

2 Peter 1: 19, "Vntill the daye dawne and the daye starre aryse in your hertes".

Tyndale also made a great impression upon the formation of English spelling. In the sixteenth century there was no right or wrong way of spelling. The variations upon the spelling for Tyndale's name, found in the letters of the government agents shuffling to and fro between England and the Continent at this time, make amusing reading; he is Tyntaell, Tandeloo, Tendalle and more besides. In the desperate haste between the printing of the fragment at Cologne and the Worms edition Tyndale made numerous changes to spelling. For example, in Matthew 5 *wen* became *when*; *mouth* became *mought*; *thers* became *theirs*; *mourne* became *morne*; *evle* became *yvell* and *evyll*; *prophetts* became *prophets*. Elsewhere, *synners* became *sinners*; *mooste* became *most*; *pierles* became *pearles*; *burthen* became *burden* and so on. But so great was the influence of his revised edition of 1534 that many of his spellings became the accepted norm.

It is rarely appreciated how heavily dependent upon Tyndale was every translation of the Scriptures up to, and including, the Authorised Version of King James. Fully ninety per cent of the Authorised Version New Testament stands virtually unaltered from Tyndale's 1534 revision (spelling excepted) and at least seventy-five per cent of the Revised Version likewise. As we have already noted, some of that ten per cent of change was not always for the better. One of the best illustrations of Tyndale's influence upon the Authorised Version will be found in the beautiful passage from Hebrews 12: 1-6, and few will suggest that the Authorised Version: "such contradiction of sinners" is a change for the better from "such speaking against him of sinners". Here it is just as it stands in the 1526 Worms edition:

> Wherfore lett vs also (seynge that we are compased with so gret a multitude of witnesses) laye a waye all that preseth vs doune/and the sinne that hangeth on vs/and let vs runne with pacience/vnto the battayle that is set before vs/lokynge vnto Jesus/the auctor and fynnyssher of oure fayth/which for the ioye that was set before hym/ abode the crosse/and despysed the shame/and is sett doune on the right honde off the trone off God. Consider therefore howe that he endured suche speakinge agaynst hym of sinners/lest ye shulde be weried and faynte in youre myndes. For ye have not resisted vnto bloud sheddynge/stryvynge agaynst sinne. And ye have forgotten the consolacion which speaketh vnto you/as vnto children: My sonne despyse nott the chastenynge of the lorde/nether faynte when thou arte rebuked of hym: For whom the lorde loveth/hym he chasteneth: yee/and he scourgeth every sonne that he receaveth.

Again, the dependence of the 1611 Authorised Version of King James upon Tyndale, is seen in the familiar John 3: 16-18:

> God soo loved the worlde/that he gave his only sonne for the entent/that none that beleve in hym/shulde perisshe: Butt shulde have everlastynge lyfe. For God sent not his sonne into the worlde/to condempne the worlde: But that the worlde through him/myght be saved. He that beleveth on hym shall not be condempned. But he that beleveth nott/is condempned all redy/be cause he beleveth nott in the name off the only sonne off God.

Even the narrative passages did not escape the close attention of the bishops in 1611. See for example the account of the shepherds in Luke 2: 8-14:

> And there were in the same region shepherdes abydinge in the felde/and watching their flocke by night. And loo: the angell of the lorde stode harde by them/and the

brightnes of the lorde shone rounde aboute them/and they were soore afrayed. And the angell sayd vnto them: Be not afrayed Beholde I brynge you tydinges off greate ioye/that shall come to all the people: for vnto you is borne this daye in the cite of David a saveoure/which is Christ the lorde. And take this for a signe: ye shall fynde the childe swadled/and layed in a manger. And streight waye there was with the angell a multitude of hevenly sowdiers/laudynge God/and sayinge: Glory to God an hye/and peace on the erth: and vnto men reioysynge.

But perhaps no passage is more beautiful than Tyndale's translation of the chapter on love. Here Tyndale chose the right word and the only significant change made by the Authorised Version was a tragic failure. Tyndale's *love* is infinitely better than the erroneous *charity*. 1 Corinthians 13:

Though I speake with the tonges of men and angels/and yet had no love/I were even as soundynge brasse: and as a tynklynge Cynball. and though I coulde prophesy/and vnderstode all secretes/and all knowledge: yee/if I had all fayth so that I coulde move mountayns oute of there places/and yet had no love/I were nothynge. And though I bestowed all my gooddes to fede the poore/and though I gave my body even that I burned/and yet have no love/it profeteth me nothynge.

Love suffreth longe/and is corteous. Love envieth nott. Love doth nott frawardly/swelleth not/dealeth not dishonestly/seketh nott her awne/is not provoked to anger/ thynketh not evyll reioyseth not in iniquitie: but reioyseth in the trueth/suffreth all thynge/beleveth all thynges hopeth all thynges/endureth in all thynges. Though that prophesyinge fayle/other tonges shall cease/or knowledge vanysshe awaye: yet love falleth never awaye.

For oure knowledge is vnparfet/and oure prophesyinge is vnperfet: but when thatt which is parfet is come: then that which is vnparfet shall be done awaye. When I was a chylde/I spake as a chylde/I vnderstode as a childe/I ymmagened as a chylde: but as sone as I was a man I put awaye all childesshnes. Nowe we se in a glasse even in a darke speakynge: but then shall we se face to face. Nowe I knowe vnparfectly: but then shall I knowe even as I am knowen. Nowe abideth fayth/hope/and love/even these thre: but the chefe of these is love.

All this provides an ample illustration of the literary licence of the sixteenth century in that even so careful and accurate translator as Tyndale can render the same word *vnparfet, vnperfet* and *vnparfectly* or *chylde* and *childe* all within the same paragraph. And this is one liberty that even Thomas More apparently allowed.

The authorities in England had done all in their power to stamp out the importing of the New Testaments. But still they came, together with other books written by Tyndale and scurrilous attacks by Roye. On 18th June, 1528 Wolsey made the first decisive move to touch the heart of the trouble. He sent orders to ambassador Hackett to demand from the Regent of the Low Countries the arrest and extradition of three heretics: Tyndale, Roye, and Richard Herman. By the middle of July the Regent apologised for being unable to find the three men in question and, to speed up the delivery, Wolsey despatched John West, a friar from Roye's old convent at Greenwich, to aid in the search.

CHAPTER 6

FUGITIVE AND OUTLAW
1527-1531

John West arrived at a convent of his order in Antwerp and
on 2nd September, 1528 sat down to make contact with
John Hackett. He was fairly close on the trail of Constantine,
a priest who had recently fled from England, for what
reason we can only guess, and hoped soon for an arrest.
But for the chief part of his mission he had few certain leads.
He had spoken to a bookbinder in the town who assured
him that many books from the Englishmen were at Frankfurt
and that, hopefully, Roye could be induced to bring the
others to Cologne to collect payment for books that the
binder would offer to buy. There they could be arrested. A
few weeks later West and another friar set out for Cologne
where West intended to change his friar's habit and lie in
wait for Tyndale and Roye.

Hackett himself had not been inactive and had already
arranged for Richard Herman to be thrown into prison,
although he was later released owing to insufficient evidence.
West apparently soon realised that the bookbinder's ruse
was more hopeful than realistic and before long he moved
on to the great Book Fair at Frankfurt. Here he met up with
Hermann Rinck, the Cologne senator who had frustrated the
first attempt at printing, and who, on Wolsey's orders, was
about the same business as West.

Clearly the cardinal was in earnest. He now had his
ambassador (Hackett), a Cologne senator (Rinck), and two
friars in civilian dress (of whom one was West), hunting for
Tyndale and Roye. On 4th October Rinck wrote to Wolsey

admitting that "Roye and Hutchins (Tyndale)" had not been seen in Frankfurt since Easter and that their printer, John Schott, had no idea where they were. Rinck contented himself with buying up and destroying all the books he could find, with the exception of two which he was sending to the cardinal by West who was returning to England. Rinck concluded, "I will make the most strenuous efforts to arrest the aforesaid Roye and Hutchins, and all other enemies and rebels against the king's grace and yours, and to find out where they live". West was ever busy; he returned to England to hunt for Roye whom he believed to be in the country; he wrote to Wolsey from the continent with certain news of the whereabouts of Tyndale at Frankfurt; then he was back in England chasing Roye again. But in all this the agents were far from their quarry.

MARBURG 1527-1529

As soon as the Worms edition of the New Testament was safely through the press, Tyndale and Roye parted company, glad to be rid of each other. It is certain, therefore, that Tyndale had nothing to do with the bitter attack upon Wolsey put out by Roye in his scurrilous poem "Rede me and be not wroth", for which Tyndale was unjustly blamed. Tyndale later dissented from having any part in the work: "It becometh not the Lord's servant to use railing rhymes, but God's Word". When Roye passed from Tyndale's company, we cannot tell for certain where he went. Foxe, the martyrologist, tells us that he died at the stake in Portugal in 1531. But where was Tyndale? It is clear that he stayed at Worms at least until April 1527 but then he moved to Marburg, a hundred miles north of Frankfurt and well off the beaten track of government agents. But Tyndale did not move here to lie low and wait for the storm to pass; that would have been all too easy. During the years that Rinck, Hackett and West were scouring the cities and interrogating the printers, Tyndale was putting through the press of John Hoochstraten a number of important works. He was fortunate to have found such a sympathetic printer who was prepared to change his identity to that of a Hans Lufft, and transfer his press from Antwerp to Marburg, in order to throw Tyndale's enemies, and biographers, off the real scent!

The *Parable of the Wicked Mammon* was the first work to which Tyndale put his name. The work is dated 8th May, 1528 and Tyndale criticised Roye and his friend Jerome for their unworthy outbursts. Based upon the parable of the unjust steward, the whole book is really an exposition of the evangelical doctrine of justification by faith. Tyndale borrowed heavily from a sermon of Luther on the same parable, but in spirit if not in letter, it was his own: "If thou wilt therefore be at peace with God, and love him, thou must turn to the promises of God, and to the gospel. . . . For faith bringeth pardon and forgiveness freely purchased by Christ's blood, and bringeth also the Spirit; the Spirit looseth the bonds of the devil, and setteth us at liberty. . . . See therefore thou have God's promises in thine heart, and that thou believe them without wavering. . . . Also remember, that his Son's blood is stronger than all the sins and wickedness of the whole world." Nothing else can save, warned Tyndale, "though thou hast a thousand holy candles about thee, a hundred ton of holy water, a ship-full of pardons, a cloth-sack full of friar's coats, and all the ceremonies in the world, and all the good works, deservings, and merits of all the men in the world, be they, or were they, never so holy". Tyndale's pen ran fast as he soared into the high realms of the reformers' great doctrines: "Christ is our Redeemer, Saviour, peace, atonement, and satisfaction to Godward for all the sin which they that repent (consenting to the law and believing the promises) do, have done, or shall do. So that if through fragility we fall a thousand times in a day, yet if we do repent again, we have alway mercy laid up for us in store in Jesus Christ our Lord."

By October of the same year Tyndale had completed his powerful, and probably most influential, book *The Obedience of the Christian Man*. The work set out to answer the charge that the reformers were rebels against lawful authority. The Peasant Revolt in Germany had lent power to the charge, and some of the language of the hot-heads, suitably embellished by the complaining friars, turned to the same end. Tyndale discussed the relationship of subject to king, servant to master, wife to husband, child to parent and in every case maintained that a true appreciation of Scripture demanded loyal obedience. But he also placed popes and prelates under the authority of the king, which was one reason why Henry did not take too much exception to this book! Tyndale went further than his immediate task. He attacked the pope as the antichrist and the Roman system as the cause of all suffering. He ridiculed the priests and their "wives", the extortion by the friars, and the idea of it being treason to say the Lord's prayer in English. At some of the recent outbursts from Fisher, Bishop of Rochester, Tyndale went as far as his mild character would allow him to. "God stop his blasphemous mouth," he cried. And Tyndale could be a master of irony when he wished. Martin Luther had publicly burnt the pope's bull of excommunication; "a manifest sign", Rochester had written, "that he would have burned the pope's holiness also, if he had had him!" Tyndale could not restrain himself from a similar argument in response: "Rochester and his holy brethren have burnt Christ's Testament; an evident sign, verily, that they would have burnt Christ Himself also, if they had had Him!"

But in this book, as much as anywhere, Tyndale showed his ability to handle the Scriptures. He was a master at exegesis. For a thousand years the Church had interpreted the two swords in Luke 22 as referring to the pope's spiritual and temporal power; it was the strong and clear mind of Tyndale that gave it the simple and only sensible meaning that the disciples required no more than two swords, for however many they had, they would all have fled by midnight. Similarly he dared to challenge the misinterpretation of Matthew 16: 18-19 and showed that Christ alone is the foundation of the Church and that binding and loosing is nothing more or less than the preaching of the Gospel. This was an interpretation, he reminded his readers, with which even the great Jerome, compiler of the Latin Vulgate, agreed. Tyndale laid down principles for interpreting Scripture with Scripture and every page of his book is liberally supported with Scripture.

The Obedience of the Christian Man breathed the Gospel, as did all his work. Referring to the value of the death of Christ he wrote, "God sent Him into the world to bless us, and to offer Himself for us a sacrifice of a sweet savour, to kill the stench of our sins, that God henceforth should smell them no more, nor think on them any more!" The poor ploughboy could understand that language plainly enough. Perhaps no book, with the exception of the New Testament itself, had such a profound influence in England at this time. One copy even found its way into the possession of Anne Boleyn.

King Henry was having difficulty with Catherine. She cried, pleaded, obstinately refused to be divorced and had no intention of retiring gracefully into a convent as the first unwanted wife of Louis XII had done. Henry could handle foreign ambassadors, his ministers, and even parliament, but he was never quite able to manage Catherine. His case had been taken to Rome and passed back; the charade of a trial had been enacted to prove the king guilty of sin in marrying Catherine, the widow of Henry's brother Arthur; the universities were being appealed to and everyone, from peasant to the archbishop, gave his verdict. The only man who remained silent was the pope, because whichever way he jumped he would fall on one great prince or another. Besides, Spanish troops had just taken Rome and imprisoned His Excellency and how could he be expected to declare the aunt of his captor, Charles V, an adulteress? And thus the sordid business dragged on.

The king brought Anne Boleyn into the court and she lent her copy of the *Obedience* to a lady in her service. The young lady was reading the book when her suitor playfully snatched it away from her, found help in what he read and refused to return it. Unfortunately he was caught reading it during divine service and the book was passed to Cardinal Wolsey. When Anne asked for the return of her book the story was blurted out by her distraught lady-in-waiting. Anne went to the king, who spoke to the cardinal, and the cardinal returned the book at once. Apparently the king "delighted in the book" and declared it to be a book "for me and all kings to read". In that at least he spoke wisely, for Tyndale had declared in the *Obedience* that women and pride were "the common pest of all princes". But perhaps His Majesty did not read that part! Thomas More disagreed with his master and called it "a holy book of disobedience". One of the most damning evidences of a heretic was the possession of Tyndale's *Obedience of the Christian Man*.

THE OLD TESTAMENT

1528 was an unhappy year in England. The king's divorce issue dragged on; Henry diverted attention by declaring a war, that nobody wanted, upon Charles V and, although he never intended to take action, the stance made him feel good. Following long years of drought the country was devastated by floods; trade ceased because of the threat of war and the Sweating Sickness returned. The king saw it all as the wrath of God against his marriage to Catherine. But Tyndale, the hunted exile living under the shadow of arrest and the stake, knowing that agents were scouring the country for him, turned his attention to the Old Testament. It says much for the disciplined mind of this lonely scholar that with the pack baying for his blood, he could calmly set himself to master Hebrew.

William had little opportunity to learn Hebrew in his homeland, for Jews had been banished from England since the reign of Edward I and there was no Hebrew professor at the universities until 1524, the year Tyndale left England. Tyndale may possibly have obtained an old Hebrew grammar and begun the study of the language in his stone and timber room in Gloucestershire. He could, of course, take advantage of the Hebrew professor at Wittenberg, which doubtless he did, but his stay there was brief and at that time he was hurrying his New Testament to its completion. Therefore Tyndale, in exile, living hand to mouth and in constant expectation of arrest, was learning Hebrew, translating and revising the New Testament, commencing

his translation of the first five books of the Old Testament
(*the Pentateuch*), and finding time to write long and valuable
books for the help of his compatriots in the homeland. All
this between 1526 and the end of 1529. How often his head
and eyes must have rebelled against the constant attention
to small letters in the half-light; how much his cramped
body must have ached in every limb and have cried out for
exercise after hours and days hunched over his desk in a
small spare room kindly lent to him by a friendly merchant!
All this was far distant from the comfortable married
quarters into which Luther had recently moved with his
newly-wed wife, Catherine. It was also very different from
Luther's large university library with a sympathetic faculty,
and the strong protecting arm of the Elector of Saxony
outside the well fortified walls of Wittenburg, a city that
would, and years later did, shed its blood in defence of the
learned doctor and his Gospel. The only comfort for Tyndale
during these urgent years of unceasing and relentless
hounding by the king's agents was the arrival of his close
and dear friend, John Frith, and the knowledge that he was
in the centre of God's will in providing a Bible for the
English speaking world.

HAMBURG AND ANTWERP 1529-1530

With his manuscripts of the *Pentateuch* carefully packed,
Tyndale ventured out of Marburg and journeyed to Antwerp
on the coast. But he could not stay here. If Antwerp lay
close to England, it also lay in the direct path of danger.
By June of the previous year a concerted effort had been
launched across the channel to track down the elusive
pimpernel and, by September, Rinck and West had passed
through Antwerp; they might well return. In January 1529
Tyndale's name was mentioned in open court as a heretic
and rebel and the following month a fresh hunt was planned.
It would be foolish to try and print the *Pentateuch* here.
Consequently, the fugitive boarded a ship to carry him
around the Frisian Islands and into the mouth of the Elbe
with the intention of landing at Hamburg. There he had

friends and a printer would not be hard to find. He would
still be sufficiently close to England for his new translation
to be hurried across the channel. The whole route avoided
the dangerous overland travel or a visit to Cologne. But
disaster awaited this way. His ship was wrecked on the coast
of Holland and all his precious manuscripts were lost.
Tyndale lost his money, valuable time, and the fruit of
months of hard labour. It appeared even more disastrous
than the discovery of his New Testament at Cologne. How
Tyndale felt as he boarded another vessel and arrived in
Hamburg is not hard to imagine.

The home of Margaret von Emmerson was always open
to the reformers. Her husband had died sometime before
1523 and his widow kept the home open. Tyndale knew
where to go once in Hamburg. The Emmerson family was
strongly Lutheran. Two of Margaret's six children went to
the University of Wittenberg and her nephew, Matthias, had
accompanied Tyndale there in 1524. Not inappropriately
Matthias later became secretary of the London Steelyard!
Here, in the Emmerson home, Tyndale burst out his story
to Miles Coverdale, a graduate whom he had known at
Cambridge. If William was cast down, the eager enthusiasm
of his friend urged him to a fresh effort. Coverdale was no
great scholar and his knowledge of languages was scant,
therefore he could provide little more than moral and
spiritual support for the great reformer. Coverdale was a
few years older than Tyndale and was to hold the double
distinction of living to the great age of eighty-one, dying
naturally in 1569, which was unusual for a faithful reformer,
and of producing the Bible that circulated by the express
command of Henry VIII. In the year of Tyndale's death,
Coverdale's Bible became the first ·complete translation of
the whole Bible to be printed in England, and its New
Testament was almost entirely Tyndale's work. But now,
with the inspiration of Coverdale at his side, Tyndale
repeated his laborious task from March until December
1529 when the *Pentateuch* was once more ready for the press.

In addition to the constant threat of discovery—and a new
and intensive search had begun in January—Hamburg was

invaded by the Sweating Sickness in June 1529. This mysterious and frightening illness swept the Continent during the latter half of the fifteenth century and the first half of the sixteenth, though its most powerful effects were felt in England where, "if the half in every town escaped, it was thought a great favour". The boiling fever carried off men, women and children without warning in a few minutes or a few hours; people fell down in the street and general panic broke out. The king hurried into the country and wrote encouraging letters to Wolsey who remained at his post in London, sniffing his spice-stuffed oranges. The disease seemed perniciously to stalk the Englishmen, and in Calais and Antwerp for example, *a Boke or Counseill Against the Sweate* claimed, "It followed Englishmen as the shadow does the body; it generally singled out English residents or visitors, whilst the native population were unaffected". And if at Calais and Antwerp, why not at Hamburg also? Within a month more than a thousand had died in the city. But, unmoved, Tyndale pressed on with his task. What was the point of fleeing from the city? If the Sweating Sickness raged within the walls of Hamburg, the king's agents lurked outside and both offered a similar fiery ordeal.

Once the *Pentateuch* was safely through the press, Tyndale felt that he must return to Antwerp. It was a post of danger, but it was only prudence and never fear that determined Tyndale's course of action. Besides, by the end of 1529 Wolsey had lost the Great Seal of Lord Chancellor. Sir Thomas More had succeeded him and parliament had met and corrected just a few of the worst abuses of clerical extortion; perhaps times would change. Tyndale settled at Antwerp, on the frontier of danger. Many of his friends like Barnes, Rogers and Coverdale, sought more secluded havens at Hamburg and Saxony; even Frith slipped over to Holland to marry a wife. But Tyndale's heart lay across the channel and at least at Antwerp he could walk down to the quay and imagine he could see the country he loved and picture John Ploughman driving his oxen across the field. Tyndale was no merchant adventurer, no roving explorer, no hot-headed zealot. He wanted only to serve England with the Book that could change the heart of a nation, and for that he considered no price too high.

Antwerp was no stranger to the preaching of the Gospel. In 1524, whilst Tyndale was busy at his translation in Wittenberg, a priest from a village called Mels, close by Antwerp, began to preach against popery. Such crowds came to hear him that he moved his pulpit to the open fields and a price was set on his head by the authorities. An Augustinian monk began to preach in Antwerp at the same time. On a particular Sunday a vast crowd gathered to hear the Gospel in a shipbuilder's yard. When the preacher failed to arrive, a young man climbed a ship's mast and, thinking it a shame that the crowd should disperse without any spiritual food, began to preach. As his reward, two butchers seized him and dragged him to the magistrates of the city who ordered him to be tied in a sack and thrown into the river. Thus the city of Tyndale's last residence engraved its name in history with the blood of the preachers of reform. But Antwerp was close by the great city of Brussels; it was here, on 14th October, 1529, that an edict was issued against the Lutherans. On 7th December, the edict was confirmed with the following grisly addition: "That nobody should presume from that time forwards to write, print, or cause to be written or printed any new book upon what subject soever, without having first obtained letters of licence for the said purpose; on pain of being piloried, and marked besides with a red-hot iron, or an eye put out, or a hand cut off according to the discretion of the judge, who is to see the sentence executed without delay or mercy". Such were the intentions of the city into which Tyndale had now moved.

THE PENTATEUCH IN ENGLAND

The *Pentateuch* was in England by the early summer of 1530, though it seems to have circulated as separate books. In the preface to this work, Tyndale gave some account of his life and work thus far and concluded by offering his work upon the altar of scholarship. Let men study it and correct it; yes, and let it be "disallowed and also burnt, if it seem worthy, when they have examined it with the Hebrew, so that they first put forth of their own, translating another that is more correct". This is typical of Tyndale's sincerity and humility. He would gladly stop work and see his translation burnt, if only someone with authority would produce something better. The truth of the matter was that there was no-one in the English speaking world that could take up the challenge. Even the literary giant, Sir Thomas More, was not merely too busy with his new office, but was not equal to Tyndale's grasp of Greek and Hebrew, still less of the mind and heart of the rustic ploughman.

It was unfortunate that Tyndale added some strong marginal notes to his *Pentateuch* for, though true, they gave the authorities all the stick they required with which to beat the reformer.

At Exodus 32: 28, where three thousand were slain after worshipping the golden calf, Tyndale commented upon the pope's decrees of excommunication: "The pope's bull slayeth more than Aaron's calf, even one hundred thousand for one hair of them".

Numbers 18: 24 (where the Levitical priests were to have no property save the tithes), "Ours will have tithe, and lands, and rents, and kingdoms, and empire and all".

Deuteronomy 6: 6 (where God commanded Israel to keep His Word in their heart), "It is heresy with us for a layman to look on God's Word or to read it".

Of the one hundred and eight such notes, not one is borrowed from Luther. This is Tyndale's heart speaking. And who will condemn him for such language when, just a few months earlier, his close friend, Thomas Hilton, had gone to the stake at Maidstone in Kent, and when, all around him in the Low Countries, men and women were being drowned, roasted, burned, buried, branded and maimed for daring to reject the corruptions of the Church?

With the Old Testament, though less than with the New, much of Tyndale's work was retained in the Authorised Version, and frequently the revisers in 1881 broke with the Authorised and returned to Tyndale. His accuracy with the Hebrew is unquestionable and many of his earthy phrases are delightful: the Lord "trounced Sisera" (Judges 4: 15); the woman "broke his brainpan" with the millstone (Judges 9: 53); the lad was an "abstainer" (Judges 13: 5, for Nazarite); God "played his pageants with them" (1 Samuel 6: 6 where the Authorised Version has "wrought wonderfully among them"); the "sheriffs of the shires"; Jezebel "starched her eyes", and so on. The Authorised Version was right not to borrow all these, but the ploughboy understood them well; they were plain everyday expressions to him.

On 25th May the king entered the Star Chamber and personally denounced *The Parable of the Wicked Mammon* and *The Obedience of the Christian Man.* Fickle Henry had forgotten that just two years earlier he was "delighted in the book"; it was now apparently "blasphemous and pestiferous". All such books were to be surrendered within fifteen days. The king promised an official translation; but this was nothing more than an empty bribe. In the same month Tunstall set fire to another bonfire of books at St Paul's Cross and preached yet another sermon, one of his last acts before the cruel Stokesley succeeded him to the bishopric of London. In the Low Countries the Emperor, Charles V, had ordered all copies of the New Testament, in any language, to be surrendered and all printing to be halted. Heretics were condemned to death: men by the sword, women by burying alive and the relapsed by fire.

Towards the end of 1530 Tyndale put forth a fierce attack upon the clergy in his *Practice of Prelates.* The clerics howled even louder. In it he also discussed the question "whether the king's grace may be separated from his queen, because she was his brother's wife". It was a dangerous issue, but everyone else had given their opinion, so why not Tyndale? With devastating simplicity, he produced one of the few sensible explanations of the two passages of Scripture the Church could not, or would not, reconcile. Leviticus 18: 16, means "that Moses forbiddeth a man to take his brother's wife as long as his brother liveth" whereas Deuteronomy 25: 5 makes it clear that "after his death it is lawful". This simple harmony no-one could reasonably dispute, except the king because it came down against his desire to have his marriage declared null and void, and the Church because she had long since decreed that a man could not marry his brother's wife under any circumstances. Pope Julius II had given Henry special license in 1509, but even Rome could not change its mind too frequently without looking foolish. Here again Tyndale showed that he was slave to no man. The Lutherans concluded that the marriage might have been invalid, but that it ought not to be dissolved at this late stage. The English reformers condemned the union and declared that it should be broken in favour of Anne Boleyn. Tyndale agreed with neither party. The marriage with Catherine was lawful and could never be broken. And Tyndale was right.

AN INVITATION TO RETURN

Every attempt to discover Tyndale had failed. It would be quite inexplicable why he was so eagerly and diligently sought, so hard at work in a most obvious place, and yet so elusive, if we did not acknowledge the hand of a sovereign God whose purposes for Tyndale were not yet complete. When the agents passed through Antwerp, Tyndale, who had no more idea of their whereabouts than they had of his, was absent. When he returned, they had passed on. Sometimes we cannot be sure where Tyndale was either, but the despatches of the agents always show them to be on the wrong track. Finally the king decided upon a new approach.

Stephen Vaughan was a merchant adventurer of Antwerp; he was known to have sympathies with the reformers and had been in the service of Thomas Cromwell, who was now rising to power in Henry's court. Vaughan left England towards the end of November 1530 (possibly on the 29th, the very day that Wolsey died of fright in the Abbey at Leicester) with a delicate mission. His task was to find the reformer and persuade him to return to England and enter the king's service! This was not so ridiculous as it might at first appear. Thomas More, the Lord Chancellor, was already in difficulty and his end could not be far away. Thomas Cromwell was a known sympathiser with reform (though not always with the reformers), and the king could usefully employ an outspoken priest with the evident gifts that

Tyndale possessed; besides it always boosted Henry's ego to have scholars at his court. If once he could persuade him to return, assure him of his kingly affection and obtain a token apology for Tyndale's past misdemeanours, the king could use his pen against the overbearing power of the Church and the absolute authority of Rome. At least William and Henry would be in agreement at one point, the supremacy of the king. But His Majesty would have to learn the hard way that he had grossly misjudged his man.

How to find Tyndale was Vaughan's first task. By the following January he had searched and enquired and had sent three letters to Tyndale, one to Frankfurt, one to Hamburg and one to Marburg, in the hope of establishing some contact. Although he lamented to his king, "My endeavours have been repeatedly brought to naught", he had at least received a reply in Tyndale's own handwriting. However, Vaughan does not appear to have known which of the three letters reached Tyndale, and besides, Tyndale's reply was evasive and untrusting. We would all like to know which letter made contact with the reformer, since he may well have been in Antwerp all the time! He had friends in each of the three other towns who would know how to divert mail back to Tyndale. Vaughan mentioned a new book that he had heard of, but he could not obtain a copy and was unsure whether or not it was yet off the press. The agent was already impressed by his elusive quarry, who, he claimed, "is of a greater knowledge than the king's highness doth take him for". But *that* was meant strictly for the eye of Cromwell; the king did not err in his judgements any more than the pope did in his.

January was the month when Henry invoked the ancient law of Praemunire (1393) which forbade any papal bulls against the crown on pain of death and confiscation of property; that was an insurance policy against the future. And he at once fined the church £100,000 retrospectively for having disobeyed it; that was the first premium. Henry added that he must be recognised as the "sole protector and Supreme Head of the Church and clergy of England"; and that was a prelude to the Act of Supremacy in 1534. The

Church, in its death throes, hit out wherever it could. A squire of Toddington in Gloucestershire, known personally to Tyndale as a learned and godly man, had proclaimed in his will a belief in salvation through Christ alone, and he rejected all other mediators or the need for anyone to pray for his soul after death. For these sentiments his body was exhumed and burnt as a heretic. In March, Latimer, Crome and Bilney were arrested. Latimer was let off, Crome recanted, but little Bilney went to the stake in August. John Frith visited England at Easter and returned with the sad news that the persecution was strengthening all over the realm. A promise of safe conduct was hardly sufficient to entice Tyndale out of hiding. John Huss had been burnt at Constance in 1415 with a safe conduct in his pocket; Luther barely escaped with his life at Worms in 1521 under the same protection, and when Barnes came to England at the end of 1531 even Thomas More muttered about setting the safe conduct aside. Stephen Vaughan would require some powerful and persuasive arguments if ever he came face to face with Tyndale.

By the end of March Vaughan was able to send the king a manuscript copy of part of Tyndale's *Answer to More*. A few weeks later, on 18th April, he could send a little more of the same book. But beyond this he had something very exciting to relate. On 17th April a messenger had approached Vaughan informing him that a certain friend would like to speak with him and that, if the agent was willing, he would conduct him to an appointed rendez-vous.

Not unnaturally Vaughan cautiously replied, "What is your friend, and where is he?"

The messenger was guarded. "His name I know not, but if it be your pleasure to go where he is, I will be glad thither to bring you."

There are times when a government agent cannot be too particular about his own safety and Stephen Vaughan followed the messenger out of the city gates and into a field lying close by Antwerp. There he was introduced to a stranger who opened the conversation with: "Do you not know me?"

"I do not well remember you," Vaughan replied some-what guardedly.

"My name," said the stranger, "is Tyndale."

From the conversation that followed it is evident that Tyndale's only purpose in this encounter with the king's agent was to protest his loyalty to the king. He spoke of his exile as "bitter absence from my friends"; and he talked of his hunger, thirst, cold and the great danger under which he constantly lived; and it was only for his love for his home-land and its sovereign. "I hope with my service," the outlaw continued, "to do honour to God, true service to my prince, and pleasure to his commons." However, to the pressing request of Vaughan to return home, Tyndale declined on the grounds that the king's promise once made could be easily broken, "by the persuasion of the clergy, which would affirm that promises made with heretics ought not to be kept". Perhaps Luther had told Tyndale that this very argument was strongly made at Worms in 1521.

Evening was drawing on and Tyndale became a little fearful that it was not altogether healthy to be in the open with a secret agent at nightfall. He drew the conversation to a close and, assuring Vaughan that he would either meet him again or hear from him soon, walked off in the direction away from the town. Stephen Vaughan, hoping for a further meeting, and realising that nothing more could be gained that night returned to the town; he was convinced that Tyndale must have slipped quietly into the city before the great gates closed for the night since there was no possibility that he should find lodgings outside. It is significant that Tyndale not only knew how to contact the agent, but he also knew his man and was prepared to trust himself to him so far. Vaughan now knew that the heretic lodged at Antwerp and he would certainly recognise him again. But Tyndale was right in his trust of the man, for Vaughan's warm apprecia-tion and strong commendation of the outlaw brought a sharp rebuke from Cromwell by the next despatch, which arrived a month later, warning him that the king was not impressed. His Majesty had decided that after all he did not want Tyndale in his realm, perceiving his "malicious,

perverse, uncharitable and indurate mind"; his books
were "most uncharitable, venomous and pestilent". Cromwell advised Vaughan to break off all relations with Tyndale,
and express his loyal affection for the king in his next letter,
"otherwise you will anger the king, check your own advance-
ment, and disappoint the hopes of myself and your other
friends". He should go and look for John Frith instead
because the king liked him.

But things were not that simple. Cromwell had added a
postscript that virtually cancelled out the king's spleen and
urged Vaughan to have more success with Tyndale. Vaughan
rather indiscreetly mentioned this in his next despatch to
the king on 20th May. He was now at Bergen, in the Netherlands, presumably on his way to Holland where he had
heard that John Frith had recently married and settled, "but
in what place I cannot tell". Poor Vaughan, if only these
reformers would keep still or remain silent. He was at least
sensible enough to admit that the marriage of Frith "may by
chance hinder my persuasions". Nevertheless he would go
to Holland and try.

The king's agent had another meeting with Tyndale, and
during the conversation Tyndale concluded: "If it would
stand with the king's most gracious pleasure to grant only a
bare text of the Scripture to be put forth among his people,
be it of the translation of what person soever shall please
his majesty, I shall immediately make faithful promise
never to write more, nor abide two days in these parts after
the same; but immediately to repair into his realm, and
there most humbly submit myself at the feet of his royal
majesty. . . ." Even allowing that Vaughan may have embellished his words a little, this is true to the spirit of the
great translator who, to his dying breath, longed for the king
to see the need for the Scripture in English, no matter who
translated it. For this reason it is fitting that so much of the
Authorised Version, which has had such a mighty influence
upon English speaking people over three and a half centuries,
should have used ninety per cent of Tyndale's New Testament, without any acknowledgement.

In June, Vaughan met Tyndale for the last time; it is

tempting to wonder who was trying to persuade whom since
the reformer had finally made up his mind. Within a few
weeks Stephen Vaughan was back in England, and Tyndale
was still the lonely fugitive of Antwerp, cold, hungry and
facing constant danger.

CHAPTER 7

RISING PERSECUTION
1531-1534

The late summer and autumn of 1531 provided a sad and ominous prelude to the coming year. Little Bilney was burnt at Norwich in August and Richard Bayfield died at the Smithfield stake in December. Two of Tyndale's close friends and loyal workers were thus gone. Bayfield had acted as a courier and on at least three occasions conveyed large consignments of books and Testaments to England. In the same month of December a leather-seller named Tewkesbury died at Smithfield. Others recanted and carried their faggot; a few, like George Constantine, gave in under torture and revealed valuable information regarding the involvement of certain ship's masters in the contraband traffic, and the secret marks used to identify the bales and boxes that contained forbidden books and Bibles.

Tyndale received the weekly reports of arrests, recantings and burnings with sorrow but never with recrimination towards those who broke under pressure. One of the greatest burdens upon the lonely exile must have been the knowledge that he had precipitated this cruel persecution by his translation and books and that many of those rotting in prison or dying in agony at the stake had willingly committed themselves to the great commission so close to his heart. The records reveal men in every station of life in conflict with the authorities for reading the English New Testament and other proscribed books: a French bookbinder, a Dutch printer, a priest, a weaver, servants, tailors, apprentices, leatherworkers, painters, and even a boy from

Colchester who died after being thrown into prison by Thomas More. The lists, complete with names and details of the charges, are almost endless. Men of rank and learning were not spared either.

From the pen of the man who later faced his own martyrdom without flinching came words of consolation and encouragement to those who had recanted. In his *Obedience of the Christian Man* Tyndale wrote, "If any man clean against his heart (but overcome with the weakness of the flesh), for fear of persecution, have denied, as Peter did, or have delivered his book, or put it away secretly; let him (if he repent), come again, and take better hold, and not despair, or take it for a sign that God hath forsaken him. For God ofttimes taketh His strength even from His very elect, when they either trust in their own strength, or are negligent to call to Him for His strength. And that doth He to teach them, and to make them feel, that in the fire of tribulation, for His word's sake, nothing can endure and abide save His work, and that strength only which He hath promised. For the which strength He will have us to pray unto Him night and day, with all instance." There were very few of these early English reformers who did not at first abjure, but many, like little Bilney, could not live with themselves afterwards; Bilney was carrying a copy of Tyndale's *Obedience* at the time of his final arrest.

THE PEN OF THOMAS MORE

The inquisition gathered momentum in 1532. Thomas More arrested everyone he could lay hands upon if he suspected them of holding the new views or possessing the heretical books. And each was asked for news about Tyndale. By the early spring Thomas More was urged to wield his pen once again against the exile over the water. It was a mark of the effectiveness of Tyndale's work that the greatest literary man in England should be urged to write against him. No greater honour could have been bestowed upon the reformer by the Church of Rome and, incidentally, no better publicity given to his views. As long ago as March 1528 Bishop Tunstall had urged More to write against Tyndale; some thought he was offered nearly five thousand pounds as an inducement, but it is to his credit that he refused payment, preferring the privilege of serving the pope. Thomas More, a layman, was provided with a special licence from the bishop to read heresy and collect heretical books without incurring the prescribed penalty! His first volume appeared in June 1529 entitled *Dialogue . . . touching the pestilent Sect of Luther and Tyndale*. The one hundred and fifty pages were claimed to have driven Tyndale from the field; nevertheless More found it necessary to return to the attack again and again. Tyndale replied in 1531 with *An Answer unto Sir Thomas More's Dialogue* and early in 1532 More came back with his *Confutation* of Tyndale's *Answer* against his *Dialogue*!

By the time he set his literary talents against Tyndale, Sir Thomas More had already written his *Utopia* (1516), the title of which coined a new word for the English language. In *Utopia* More set out, in fine Latin, the ideal state. In this brilliant work More showed himself to be, in many ways, far ahead of his time, with government by popular election and communal sharing unequalled by a modern socialist state; it is instructive to note, however, that although in theory Sir Thomas allowed freedom of belief in his ideal state there was absolutely no place within it for reformers. More claimed he would sooner allow a Turkish mission in Christendom than heretics! More's *Confutation* of Tyndale was a massive work. Books 1-3 came out in 1532 and a further five in 1533. Every line and letter of Tyndale was analysed and, though it may have excelled Tyndale in prosaic style, the sheer volume was more than the ordinary reader could cope with. One of More's friends estimated that he answered Tyndale with words at the ratio of twenty to one, and at times even forty to one! More's *Confutation* was a restatement of the orthodox Roman Catholic position. Against Tyndale's view of Sola Scriptura, More maintained that it was the Church that made the Scriptures and he was at pains to point out that the authority of the Church, in all its teaching, was as infallible as the Scripture itself. The Church is the Word of God unwritten whilst the Scripture is the Word of God written: "the Word of God unwritten is of as great

authority, as certain, and as sure, as is His word written in
the Scripture". More had no satisfactory explanation to
resolve the problem of what happens when the two are in
complete contradiction. In reply to Tyndale's challenge on
this very point More lamely concluded that God "is at His
liberty still and ever still shall be, to teach his truths more
and more . . . in divers ages after divers manners . . .".
All of which amounted to the claim that there is no final
resting place for truth and that it may constantly change –
if the Church says it does. More believed in continuous
revelation: "and we say also that God hath daily stirred up
and daily doth stir up new prophets in sundry parts of his
Catholic Church, holy doctors and preachers. . .". Besides,
the chancellor concluded, the Scripture is a thing far too
hard and complicated for anyone to understand without
years of learning behind him. What then is the use of
Scripture to the layman? He cannot understand it.

On the issue of purgatory More touched at the very
heart of Reformation teaching without, apparently, realising
it. In reply to Tyndale's complaint that for three-halfpence
a man could purchase an indulgence that would release the
soul from purgatory and the fires of torment, More simply
retaliated that according to Tyndale's teaching "such bare
faith and slight repentance putteth out that fire (the fires of
hell) without the cost of a penny". With the exception of the
word "slight", this was precisely the difference between
Rome and the reformers. On the subject of images More
naively admitted, "good folk which worship images of
Christ and His Saints do worship thereby Christ and His
Saints whom these images represent"; but Englishmen were
reading Exodus 20: 4-5 in Tyndale's translation of the
Pentateuch!

Tyndale had once penned his beautiful definition of the
true Church: "I say that Christ's elect Church is the whole
multitude of all repenting sinners that believe in Christ, and
put their trust and confidence in the mercy of God, feeling in
their hearts that God for Christ's sake loves them and will be,
or rather is, merciful unto them, and forgiveth them their
sins of which they repent. . . ." "No!" claimed the Lord

Chancellor, and offered his own definition: "The very
Church is . . . the common known Catholic people, clergy,
lay folk, and all which, whatsoever their language be, do
stand together and agree in the confession of one true
catholic faith, with all old holy doctors and saints, and good
Christian people beside that are already passed this fifteen
hundred years before, against . . . all the rabble of . . .
erroneous heretics". Tyndale spoke of a company, chosen and
forgiven and related to God by their faith in His mercy;
More spoke of an army, fighting against the opposition and
related to the old doctors by adherence to a creed.

That More hated Tyndale's New Testament is plain; it
was, he considered, "well worthy to be burned". Even
before the *Confutation*, Tyndale had defended his change of
those offensive words such as *penance, charity, confession* and
priest, and More, on the grounds of scholarship, conceded
Tyndale's right to do so but then shifted his ground of attack.
When reminded that his good friend Erasmus had also
changed some of those very words, More concluded that
Erasmus may rightly do so if he wished because he was
"good and faithful" but Tyndale was bent upon heresy and
therefore any change he made must be suspect.

In a more earthy vein, More could never help but despise
the reformers, some of whom gave up their ignorant vows of
celibacy and married. Unfortunately he could never level
his finger at Tyndale here, though when Tyndale in-
cautiously wrote of the possibility of a woman being allowed
to celebrate communion, More could not resist the jibe: "he
beginneth now by likelihood to look toward wedding, he
speaketh like a wooer . . . but because he is a priest and
hath promised to perpetually live chaste he will none whore
therefore, but rather will do as Luther hath done, wed a
nun and make her a whore". More hated Luther for marrying the ex-nun Catherine von Bora. It is a mark of the sad
weakness of his great mind that More totally ignored the
fact that all around him there were bishops, and abbots,
friars and monks who lived openly with their concubines
and mistresses. The popes were renowned for this. But when
any reformer, none of whom was ever accused of such gross

immorality, renounced his old vows, made in ignorance and often under pressure, and lawfully took a wife then More was enraged. For the Lord Chancellor it was better for a priest to live with a harlot than with a wife.

More hated what he called the "evangelical brethren" and their "evangelical doctrine" and, though elsewhere he protested his leniency to those arrested so that they received not so much as "a fillip on the forehead", his *Confutation* complained that too few had been burned: "but there should have been more burned by a great many than there have been within this seven years past". To burn their body in the hope of saving their soul was, he maintained, a kindly death. In his long and tedious treatise More adequately expressed the view of the Church of Rome on almost every issue of significance and presumably, since as recently as 1935 Thomas More was canonised as a "saint", he still does.

THE NET TIGHTENS

When the king threw off any hope of persuading Tyndale to return to England as a penitent subject, he determined to gain his person as a pestilent heretic. Henry ordered his new ambassador at the German court to place an urgent request before the Emperor, Charles V, that Tyndale should be handed over. Unfortunately the way Catherine was being treated in England hardly made her nephew likely to accede to any demand from Henry, and besides it was doubtful if Charles could find Tyndale any more than Henry could. The Emperor sent back a polite note to the effect that he had no evidence that Tyndale had offended the laws of his or anyone else's realm. If the Emperor knew of Tyndale's views on the legitimacy of Catherine's marriage to Henry, and he must have done, this was an added reason for his reluctance to hand him over to the king.

But Henry was not so easily thwarted. If a princely approach and a lawful request were ignored, there were other methods available. Sir Thomas Elyot would find Tyndale, kidnap him and deliver him to the king. Elyot was aware of the difficulty of his task for, as he wrote to the duke of Norfolk on 14th March, 1532, "his person (is) uncertain to

come by". Elyot spent the king's money freely in bribes; he
spent days and weeks making enquiries, loitering around the
print houses and gossiping with traders, but he was no more
successful than Rinck, Hackett, West or Vaughan and by
June Elyot resigned his post and returned to England. He
had failed his first and only major assignment as ambassador.

Added to all his other trials, Tyndale was saddled with yet
another troublesome companion in the person of George
Joye. Joye had fled from Cambridge in 1527 and some time
during the early 1530's attached himself to Tyndale, more
likely to gain some reflected glory than for any other reason.
He was a man once referred to as having "little learning and
less sense, who nevertheless considered himself equal to the
great reformer in scholarship, wisdom and ability". In the
course of time he accused Tyndale of a poor ability in Greek
and of a slavish adherence to Luther in his *Exposition on the
Sermon on the Mount*; in both cases we can be the judge and
give a decided lie to Joye's petty abuses. He was indiscreet
and hasty and lacked the mature judgement of the reformer.
The intemperate language of some of his work and letters
caused great pain to Tyndale who was often tarred with the
brush of his troublesome companion. He even accused
Tyndale of an inordinate pride. To crown everything, Joye
had the audacity to accuse the tireless translator of indolence
and gave this as his reason for issuing a private revision of
the New Testament in 1534: "All this long while Tyndale
slept, for nothing came from him so far as I could perceive".
Such ridiculous nonsense is its own condemnation.

As the net closed Tyndale became more elusive; it is likely
he remained in Antwerp throughout this year and, fearing
arrest at any moment, pursued his exposition on the Sermon
on the Mount (Matthew 5-7) and pressed on with his long
promised revision of the New Testament. News from
England was as black as ever. In January Thomas Benet was
burnt in Devonshire; in March Hugh Latimer was humilia-
ted before convocation and forced to recant; James Bayn-
ham, who abjured in February but full of remorse walked
into the church of Austin Friars on Sunday morning with a
copy of Tyndale's New Testament and *Obedience of the*

Christian Man in his hands, died at Smithfield in April.
Old Thomas Harding was burnt at Chesham during the
early summer. Thus in just over two years, during the
Chancellorship of Sir Thomas More, there had been ten
fires that are certainly known to history; others may have
died at the stake or in the foul prisons, and hundreds were
still incarcerated with little hope of release. Many of them
were plain working men and women like Edward Freese, a
young painter from Colchester, who was sent to prison for
adding a few Scripture texts to the border of a picture he
was commissioned to paint in a home, and whose pregnant
wife was kicked and beaten when she tried to visit him.
One by one Tyndale's loyal friends and men true to the
Word of God were snatched away. But worse was to come.

JOHN FRITH

Why John Frith ventured into England in July of this black
year we shall probably never know. Certainly he planned
to visit the prior of an abbey near Reading, but the business
must have been urgent to have enticed him from the com-
parative safety of Holland and the comfort of his young
wife's presence. Frith was a brilliant scholar whom even
Henry longed to have in his court and he lamented that the
young man's learning was being used to further those
"venomous and pestiferous works, erroneous and seditious
opinions of the said Tyndale".

At Reading Frith was arrested and, refusing to give his
name, was taken for a vagabond and placed in the town
stocks. How long he remained here is uncertain, but when
he was almost dead with hunger and cold he sent for Leonard
Cox the local schoolmaster who was himself a man of
considerable learning and, even more important, a friend
of Erasmus. Frith talked with him and charmed the schoolmaster with his ability in Latin and Greek and his long
quotations from Homer's *Iliad* in classical Greek. Cox, still
without gaining Frith's name, went at once to the local
magistrates who released the vagabond and sent him on his
way.

John Frith was born at Westerham in Kent in 1503 and lived most of his childhood in the nearby town of Sevenoaks where his father was an innkeeper. After an education at Eton and Cambridge, Frith entered Wolsey's new Cardinal's College at Oxford as a Junior Canon in 1525. Whilst at Cambridge, and later in London also, he met Tyndale by whose instruction, Foxe tells us, "he first received into his heart the seeds of the Gospel". By 1528 the quantity of New Testaments and other forbidden books at Oxford led to the general heresy hunt which resulted in the arrest of Frith and many of his friends. Three of these young men died whilst imprisoned in the sickly stench of the Cardinal's fish cellars beneath the college, a few abjured, one was pardoned, and John Frith was released by Wolsey on condition that he stayed away from Oxford. He did, and sailed to the Continent. Just when he joined forces with Tyndale we cannot be sure, but it is certain that his evident abilities as a scholar and his warm character (more pleasant than either Roye's or Joye's) made him a welcome companion of the lonely exile. He may have arrived in time to help Tyndale in the translation of the Pentateuch and the book of Jonah. Among his own works, Frith translated a tract by Luther and one by Patrick Hamilton, the noble Scots martyr who died at the stake in St. Andrews in 1527 and who, according to John Knox, may be called the herald of the Scottish Reformation. By the middle of 1531 Frith had prepared a powerful book on purgatory in answer to Fisher, More, and More's barrister son-in-law, Rastell. An accomplished Greek and Latin scholar, Frith chided More for making no use of either the Greek or Latin texts of Erasmus in his arguments; but to be fair, how could he? For no-one could find a case for purgatory in the New Testament. Rastell replied to Frith's book and the reformer's answer to Rastell was composed in the prison that lay at the end of this road from Reading.

After his release from the stocks at Reading, Frith made his way to London where, for a while, he enjoyed fellowship with the small knots of reformers meeting at Bow Lane and elsewhere, in warehouses, tailor's shops, private homes, in fact anywhere and everywhere and always in fear for their liberty. But the authorities soon learned that a valuable prize was astray in London and a search was made. Frith tried desperately to make his way to the coast, changing his disguise frequently and moving back and forth to escape detection. At last he was arrested at Milton Shore, near Southend in the county of Essex, by the officers of Stokesley, the fearsome Bishop of London. Frith was dragged back to London and thrown into the Tower. Apparently the prior and others were taken at the same time.

Cromwell was anxious that Frith should be made to recant, for he was a man of ability and too valuable a life to throw away unnecessarily. The lieutenant of the Tower was ordered to give Frith some liberty and not to refuse the visits of his friends. And so for five months the reformer was neglected. He was fortunate at this time to have any liberty. Poor Bayfield, before his martyrdom, was fixed to the wall by the neck, waist and legs and left in this solitary confinement and pitch darkness for days on end.

Friends came in and out of the cold cell, bringing a little comfort and risking their own liberty. Frith discussed his views of the Lord's Supper with one who pressed him for help on the matter; the clear opinions of the reformer were so helpful that the friend urged him to put an outline of his views in writing. Foolishly Frith agreed and his end was then virtually sealed. The friend unwittingly passed this paper to William Holt, a tailor who pretended sympathy with the reformers. Holt took the incriminating evidence to Thomas More immediately. However, More's system of civil investigation was so efficient that by the time Holt triumphantly arrived with his paper, the Chancellor had already received two copies of the original! More wrote a reply which he published in December. He railed at Frith for maintaining "as these other beasts do" (Wycliffe, Tyndale, Zwingli), that the bread is nothing more than bread, and the whole feast is merely a symbolic picture of the shed blood and broken body of Christ. Frith sat down in his cell to compose a reply. He wrote of himself a little later as "a man bound to a post"; he was not allowed books to aid his

reply and such pen, ink and paper as he possessed were
obtained secretly and had to be hurriedly "conveyed out of
the way" whenever the lieutenant's key rang in the lock.
And so with a mind constantly distracted, he apologised for
the shortcomings of his letters from prison.

Tyndale had meanwhile heard of his friend's arrest and
hurriedly despatched a letter to him. He addressed it to
"Dearly beloved brother Jacob", presumably to delay
identification of the recipient should the courier be inter-
cepted. Tyndale was himself a prisoner, with the only
exception that he could leave his lodging in Antwerp
whenever he felt it safe to do so. He urged Frith to remain
loyal and faithful to the true Gospel and to avoid, at all
costs, involvement in the controversy over the sacrament of
the Lord's Supper. This was the one issue upon which the
reformers were deeply divided and Frith would be wise not
to side with either Luther or Zwingli. But the warning came
too late – Frith was already committed.

Tyndale continued with general news, remarked on the
trouble he was having with George Joye and urged his
friend, "Cleave fast to the rock of the help of God, and
commit the end of all things to him". The great translator
could not refrain from an exhortation that, should the opportunity arise, Frith should thrust into his arguments the need
for Scripture to be in the mother tongue. Keep to the main
issues, the wise counsellor continued, and avoid secondary
matters of mere opinion. If you are sure you are right, and
another man is of an opposite mind, but the matter is of no
major significance to the heart of the Gospel, "you will laugh
and let it pass, and refer the thing to other men, and stick
you stiffly and stubbornly in earnest and necessary things".
Tyndale, as in so many things, was well ahead of an age that
would rack and burn a man for disagreeing over a jot or
tittle. The letter contains a delightful expression of Tyndale's
contempt of himself and love for his younger friend. He
himself is "ill-favoured in this world, and without grace in
the sight of men, speechless and rude, dull and slow-witted.
Your part shall be to supply that (which) lacketh in me."
Before closing, the exile reported on the appearance in

Antwerp of a certain John Tisen, with a red beard and black-reddish hair. Once a student under Tyndale at university he was now in the employ of Stokesley, Bishop of London. Tisen did not join the English community in the town, continued Tyndale, and had since disappeared. There is little doubt what quarry this "ambassador secret" was seeking. However, "He is our God, if we despair in ourselves, and trust in Him" concluded the fugitive from the red-bearded agent, "and he is the glory. Amen."

Whilst this letter came too late to prevent the confrontation, it did help Frith to frame his reply, and he followed the sound advice of Tyndale and conducted his case as coolly as he could. In his reply to More, John Frith sprang to the defence of his friend and explained why he and Tyndale must go on with their work until a true reformation was achieved and there was "sufficient instruction for the poor commoners". "The Word of God boileth in my body like a fervent fire," he declared, "and will needs have an issue, and break out when occasion is given . . . grant that the Word of God . . . may go abroad in our English tongue . . . and my brother William Tyndale and I have done, and will promise you to write no more." The little book comprising of Frith's reply was smuggled across to Antwerp but the author was dead before it came off the press.

John Frith used those five months to good effect; he wrote letters and treatises and was so successful that even the extraordinary John Rastell, printer, lawyer, adventurer, dramatist, military engineer, and would-be coloniser of North America, was converted to the views of the reformer; what made this even more damning for Frith was the fact that John Rastell was son-in-law to Sir Thomas More!

In January 1533 Henry secretly married Anne Boleyn, and in February he abolished Rome as the final court of appeal for any matters affecting England. At once Convocation met and decided that no pope could sanction a marriage with a brother's widow, Julius II was wrong in 1509. Henry VIII, whom Convocation decided was right all along, ordered an extravagant coronation for the young girl from Sussex and laughed when Pope Clement threatened excommunication. Princess Elizabeth was born to Henry and Anne in September. Perhaps times would change. Certainly Frith gained a little more liberty and was even allowed to leave the Tower, provided he returned before the main gate was closed for the night. But Henry had not changed, and when a royal chaplain, preaching before him, declaimed against the lack of concern in bringing to trial a young man lodged in the Tower for heresy, the king sent for Cromwell and Cranmer and asked what they were going to do about the matter. Cranmer, who had been installed as Archbishop of Canterbury in March, sent an officer and a porter to walk Frith from London to the archbishop's palace at Croydon.

The three men left the Tower and stopped for a meal at Lambeth Palace where the officer urged Frith to reconsider his position, no doubt on Cranmer's instruction, for the archbishop was already strongly inclined to the principles of the Reformation. Frith had a wife and young family overseas and a little change of stance now could make him more useful later. This line of argument had beguiled many a young reformer. The small party set out on the five hour walk to Croydon and as they came up the wooded slope of Brixton Hill another, more direct offer was put to the prisoner. Knowing that Kent bristled with friends of reform, the two guards were willing to hang back a little in order to give Frith an opportunity of escaping into the woods on the left of the road. They would give him time to make good his escape into Kent and, after a reasonable interval, they would return to Brixton village and alert the magistrates, assuring them that he had run off into the woods on the right towards Wandsworth. Frith required no time to consider his reply. All the while he had been a free man, he considered it his right to remain free and avoid arrest; but now he was the king's prisoner and had business to do at Croydon. To the amazement of his escort John Frith replied, "If you should both leave me here, and go to Croydon declaring to the bishops that you had lost Frith, I would surely follow after as fast as I might, and bring them news that I had found and brought Frith again". There was nothing more to be said and the three men arrived, just before nightfall, in Croydon where Frith slept in the porter's lodge.

The following day Frith was arraigned before his judges who included Cranmer, and the prisoner's old tutor, Gardiner. Calmly and without wavering the reformer refused the invitation to change his views about the Lord's Supper, declaring that he condemned no-one else's view providing he had the liberty of conscience to believe his own. But the sixteenth century and the Church of Rome did not understand the value of the freedom of conscience, that was one of the issues over which the fiery battle of the Reformation was fought. Cranmer had no alternative but to hand Frith back to Stokesley who, on June 17th, tried him at St. Paul's Cathedral and handed him over to Sir Stephen Peacock, Mayor of London, for the inevitable punishment. For the next two weeks John Frith lay in the stinking atmosphere of Newgate gaol. Here, loaded with chains and shivering in the gloom he continued to write by the aid of a flickering candle. Two or three visitors arrived to cajole or frighten him into submission, but Frith was ready for the end. A tailor's apprentice from Faversham in Kent, twenty-four year old Andrew Hewet was thrown into the same cell and when Frith enquired the new inmate's crime, the young man informed him that the bishop had asked him what he thought of the sacraments. When he replied, "I think as Frith does," the Bishop of London smiled and assured him he would be burnt with him. "I am content," was the bold rejoinder, and here he was. The two men had at least a few days of encouragement together before the end came.

Another letter came from Tyndale, but it may not have arrived in time. There was no need for caution now, he wrote to "Dearly beloved brother John". Knowing what the outcome must be he urged him to stand firm, remembering, "Your cause is Christ's Gospel, a light that must be fed with the blood of faith. . .". Scripture upon Scripture tumbled from his pen and all to comfort and encourage his friend. With touching thoughtfulness he concluded, "Sir, your wife is well content with the will of God, and would not, for her sake, have the glory of God hindered".

On July 4th, 1533 the two men were taken under strong escort from Newgate to Smithfield and tied to a post back to back. Dr Cook, the rector of a London Church, warned the crowd that always gathered for a good burning not to pray for them any more than they would for a dog. Frith called upon God to forgive the poor man and a torch was put to the pile of dry sticks. The wind mercifully blew the flames across Andrew Hewet and he died quickly, but that mercy for Hewet meant agony for Frith. He held out his arms to embrace the flames; they licked at his body, slowly scorching his flesh until the blackened form slumped forward at the stake.

THE HOME OF THOMAS POYNTZ

On hearing the news of his friend's death William Tyndale must have sobbed bitterly at the throne of God. Tyndale was no hard and callous leader for whom men were but pawns in a great battle of opinions; he loved all men, and the evangelical men above all. Some, like John Frith, were heart and bone to him and he had longed to see his mantle fall upon the shoulders of this younger man when his own end came. And that could not be far away. Not only was Tisen the red-beard still possibly lurking somewhere in the shadows of Antwerp, but persecution on the continent had quickened its pace recently. Four had died at Lille in Flanders, and one at Liège, all on May 3rd. At Rouen persecution was intense, and at Paris five doctors had been "taken for the Gospel". Tyndale knew of all this, for he had informed Frith of it in order to assure him that he was not alone. What was worse yet, two had died on that fateful May 3rd in the very town of Antwerp, "unto the great glory of the gospel".

However, the Reformation was spreading rapidly across the Low Countries and no persecution could successfully check it. At the Diet of Augsburg in 1530 Charles V ordered his Electors to stop the Gospel preaching. Three, including Luther's protector, Johann the Steady, flatly refused to do so; one even knelt down and offered his neck to the Emperor's sword rather than acquiesce. Charles, not used to such passive rebellion, changed the subject. So widespread and

far-reaching were the effects of the evangelical Gospel that
at the beginning of 1533 a group of Antwerp citizens
petitioned the Chancellor of Brabant to take more effective
action to alter the course of events. They complained bitterly
of the monks and nuns and preachers who had left their
orders and were running from house to house praying and
holding services. Wherever possible they listed the names of
offending churches, clergymen, civil officers and printers.
Printers always gave them trouble. They were the scourge of
the Roman Church and one of the greatest human causes for
the success of the Reformation. Without the printers the
Church could have contained the heresies, as she did with
the lollards of John Wycliffe. The loyal citizens of Antwerp
informed the Chancellor of Brabant of a printer dwelling in
the Camerstrate, just inside the old gate "next to the Vette
Henne, on the same side, towards the churchyard of our
Lady" – there could be no mistaking it! "There shall you
find books full of heresy in the English tongue, and also
others; but you must go into the chamber within; and open
the chests; there you shall find them. And the better to do
so, take with you a Christian Englishman (presumably to
masquerade as a reformer). And this printer will also show
you a great heretic and doctor, who for this heresy has been
driven out of England." That was Tyndale. "We beg you to
act," the citizens concluded, "we have given you material
enough. Do as they have done in Spain; purge the town.
Strengthen the laws; make half-yearly searches after heretics.
We write because our spiritual and lay heads have no care
for these things."

Some response must have been forthcoming, for the letter
was laid before the council in January. The queen regent
was informed and within weeks some of those named in the
letter were disciplined. In March a priest was arrested, taken
to Vilvorde castle and the following year burnt at Brussels.
On May 3rd the two laymen were executed. What became
of the particular printer we do not know, but Tyndale
himself must have seen the end not far away. His printer and
regular haunt were now known. But we can also appreciate
the growing number of friends of the Gospel; more and more

Waterfront and city centre of Antwerp

were ready to shield the great translator and he could move from home to home when he felt the authorities or agents were closing in. But in the numerical strength of those favourable to reform lay the weakness that finally cost Tyndale his liberty and life. It is easier for a betrayer to slip into a crowd.

Sometime in the early part of 1534 Tyndale was invited to live in the home of the English merchants in Antwerp. Whilst his whereabouts would no longer be concealed, he could enjoy considerable protection here, for the house had been devoted to the use of the merchants for more than sixty years and it was virtually accorded diplomatic status so that it became a little piece of England; it was Antwerp's equivalent to the London Steelyard. Since the English traders brought considerable wealth into the town, the authorities were always anxious to remain on friendly terms with these foreign businessmen. Provided he stayed close to the great house, Tyndale would have little to fear, and the merchants offered him a generous stipend which meant that for the first time in his life he was comfortably settled. Tyndale had earned nothing from all his labours thus far. Royalties and copyright were unknown until the eighteenth century, and an author or translator could expect no automatic payment. He normally dedicated his work to some rich nobleman and hoped for a reward! Since Tyndale wrote for the poor there was little he could expect in return.

Thomas Poyntz was a member of the grocers' company and a relative of Lady Walsh of Little Sodbury. Tyndale had met Poyntz in London back in 1523 and already the grocer was heavily involved with the views of the Steelyard men. With this family Tyndale now settled in the English House. At last the shadow, slipping from house to house and passing furtively down the narrow streets with frequent backward glances, becomes a real man once more and we know how he lived and where. The coded messages, silent couriers and secret rendez-vous are almost a thing of the past. Tyndale was among friends, strong friends. But one small indiscretion could yet prove fatal.

When he came into the Poyntz home, Tyndale was thin

and none too strong. His frugal and anxious life, together
with the rigid discipline of his study, had taken its toll upon
his health. But Mistress Poyntz would soon change all that with
comfortable hospitality and good food. Tyndale's time was
still well disciplined. He reserved two days in the week which
he called his pasttime. On Monday he visited all the English
exiles, who had been forced out of their homeland for the
sake of conscience. He enquired after their welfare, encouraged them and supplied some of their needs out of his
generous allowance. On Saturday he wandered the town,
poking in every hovel and alley to discover the poor and
diseased and, wherever he found genuine cases of hardship,
would supply their needs also. Quite apart from the evident
risk he took in travelling the city so freely and alone, his
practical care stands monumentally above the railing prelates in England.

It must ever stand to the honour of Tyndale's name that
even his most bitter enemy and most prejudiced opponent
could never find one fault, real or imagined, to lay to his
charge. The one exception to this may be considered his
companion George Joye; but Joye's character was so suspect,
his actions so unchristian, and his accusations so universally
rejected as absurd, that we may dismiss him at once. Joye's
petty complaints stand alone against the united testimony of
friend and foe alike. The isolated bleating of one black sheep
does not mean that the whole flock is lost. Thomas More
had long ago admitted Tyndale to be "a man of sober and
honest living (who) looked and preached holily". His only
fault, even to More, was his Gospel. But even compared with
his fellow reformers Tyndale stands out. His words may be
strong and sharp at times, but they were never scurrilous or
cruel; however ill-treated he never railed in return, and his
strongest words were in defence of his friends, not himself.

For sheer honesty, Tyndale had no equal. The sixteenth
century was the age of the princely lie. Henry lied blatantly
and even Cardinal Wolsey could lie to the face of Fisher,
Bishop of Rochester, without blushing; the popes lied,
everybody lied, even Erasmus encouraged a companion, "Do
not mind telling a lie or two in a friend's interest". Sadly,

many of those early reformers were not wholly honest. George Joye admitted that once when asked where he was lodging, "I was so bold to make the scribe a lie for his asking," and having sent his pursuers on a fool's errand, made his escape to the continent. Dr Barnes made an elaborate charade of having committed suicide by drowning, to the extent of leaving a suicide note, in order to gain time to make his way to the coast and thence over the channel to safety. And even John Frith had earlier jumped his parole. In their day these were "trifles" and few were in a position to criticise them. But not even such "trifles" could be found in the life of Tyndale. He was a man wholly true to his God and the Gospel. Foxe, who was in a position to obtain his information directly from Thomas Poyntz, described him as: "A man without any spot or blemish of rancour or malice, full of mercy and compassion, so that no man living was able to reprove him of any sin or crime".

The sixteenth century was also the age of invective when no man's character was safe from the bitterest abuse of his enemy's pen. There were no laws of libel and no holds barred. If there had been but one chink in Tyndale's holy character, we can be sure that his enemies would have exploited it. But they were totally unable to criticise him and this simple fact is the greatest proof of Tyndale's likeness to the One whose Book he was so eager to give to all England.

For the remainder of each week Tyndale laboured at his books. And when Sunday came he went to the home of one merchant or another where a small company assembled. There he read the Scriptures, in a way that came, as one observer described it, "so fruitfully, sweetly and gently from him, much like to the writing of John the evangelist, that it was a heavenly comfort and joy to the audience to hear him read the Scriptures". Thomas More was right when he complained that Tyndale no longer said mass or followed the customary rituals in any church. Why should he? He had long since passed from the dead letter to the life-giving Spirit; and there was true spiritual life amongst Thomas Poyntz and many of his fellow merchants. The chaplain at the English House was a man named John Rogers. He was no friend of

the reformers when he first came to Antwerp and it may seem
strange that he should have been invited at all. But by no
means all the merchants were touched by the new doctrines
and perhaps Rogers was accepted as a suitable compromise
and counter-balance to Tyndale. However this may be, it was
not long before he fell under the influence of Tyndale and his
New Testament and by 1535 Rogers was a loyal friend of
Tyndale. This was the John Rogers who produced Matthew's
Bible in 1537, the New Testament of which was wholly
Tyndale's with only insignificant changes.

A REVISED NEW TESTAMENT

Here in the home of Thomas Poyntz and his hospitable wife,
Tyndale completed his revision of the New Testament and
sent it across the channel in 1534. One brave and enterprising
printer in Antwerp, Christopher van Endhoven, had already
put through his press at least four editions of the New
Testament and he personally took charge of the operation of
smuggling the copies into England and distributing them.
His contact man was John Row, a French book-binder who
was led to Smithfield in 1531 and forced to throw his books
on the fire. Endhoven was arrested in the same year and
imprisoned at Westminster where he died. In spite of the
fact that at least two of these reprints were full of errors,
since Tyndale was presumably at Hamburg at the time and
had no opportunity to correct the Belgian printer's mistakes,
the editions sold out by the end of 1533. But Tyndale would
not be hurried. His revision was to be painstakingly thorough.
This annoyed George Joye who was persuaded by the
printers to correct the type of a new edition. He was paid
twelve shillings for the work, but there proved to be so many
errors that, on reflection, Joye complained he should not
have undertaken it for five times that amount. In defence of
Joye's action it should be stated that the printers were
evidently set on going ahead with or without him and he
did at least refrain from adding his or Tyndale's name
anywhere, stating merely that it had been "diligently
overseen and corrected". It was printed by the widow of
Christopher van Endhoven. But beyond this his action was

without defence. He knew that Tyndale's revision would be ready very shortly, though evidently communication between the two men was breaking down. "What Tyndale doth," he complained, "I wot not; he maketh me nothing of his counsel".

What really distressed Tyndale, however, was the fact that Joye introduced a few changes into the text by comparing it with the Latin Vulgate, for he was fairly ignorant of Greek; at a number of places he altered Tyndale's correct *resurrection* into the phrase *life after this*. It was typical of Joye that he would cause dissention and unrest over the issue of what happened to the soul of the Christian immediately after death; for a few years he had been debating the issue whilst Tyndale was urging him to let the matter drop as being non essential and a cause of division amongst the brethren. Here was Joye laying down the gauntlet with a translation that left Tyndale with no alternative but to insert a disclaimer into his own revision of 1534 lest any should consider Joye's work his own. Tyndale held the view that though the body would rise before the judgement day, "I do not think that the souls of the righteous departed are yet in full glory with Christ". However, he was ready to believe they were if Scripture could be shown to teach this; but with far greater issues at hand he had no wish to divide the brethren on such a point. Tyndale declared his desire never to cause strife over opinions, never to gain a personal following and never to translate for any other motive than to lead men to faith in Christ and to a holy life in consequence. He was eminently successful in each area. Tyndale's mind was too large to become engrossed in the details of secondary matters or embroiled in the ensuing battles; similarly, though men talked of the Lutherans and Zwinglians, the word *Tyndalians* can be found only once in the contemporary writings and it was evidently soon dropped as being wholly inaccurate. But more than anywhere Tyndale was successful in leading men to faith in Christ, and all England owed a heavy debt to the man who gave it the Gospel in the English New Testament.

In spite of the many errors in his hastily edited version, Joye persisted in issuing a further unaltered edition in

January 1535. For good measure he also published an attack
upon Tyndale. He was a man of small mind and it would
have been happier for everyone if he had never left Cambridge. His only value was to demonstrate how restrained
Tyndale could be when goaded and jibed by a fool. The
whole issue was a sordid prelude to Tyndale's finest and most
enduring monument – his 1534 New Testament. It was this
revision that eventually became ninety per cent of the King
James Authorised Version of 1611. To cite just two examples,
Westcott claims that nine-tenths of the Authorised Version
of I John and five-sixths of Ephesians belongs to Tyndale!

In his 1534 revision Tyndale placed a short explanatory
prologue before each book, with the exception of Acts and
Revelation. The text included cross references and marginal
notes (glosses). These notes were helpful and moderate and
the severity of the *Pentateuch* glosses had gone. At I Thessa-
lonians 4: 11 ("Study to be quiet, and to meddle with your
own business, and to work with your own hands") he
permitted the terse remark "a good lesson for monks and idle
friars", but most of his notes were in a more positive vein.
Perhaps with his old friend Joye in mind, he wrote beside
I Peter 4: 8 ("Love covereth the multitude of sins"), "Hate
maketh sin of every trifle, but love looketh not on small
things, but suffereth all things". The passages from the Old
Testament and the Apocrypha that were used in the
Salisbury service-book were also included so that the
worshipper could actually use his English New Testament
for the church service.

This was no casual revision, like Joye's, for Tyndale made
some four thousand changes from his 1526 edition. They are
almost all improvements, some great but most small; and he
was concerned with both sense and style. The use of *senior*
gave way to *elder* and *health* to the more proper *salvation* and
so on. Many changes in style were helpful:

Matthew 5: 9   "Blessed are the peace-makers" (1526 –
                  maintainers of peace).
Matthew 8: 26   "O ye of (endued with) little faith."
Matthew 11: 29   "And ye shall find rest (ease) unto your
                  souls."

John 1: 1   "In the beginning was the (that) word,
and the (that) word was with God, and
the word was God (God was that word)."

Hebrews 12: 16   "Esau, which for one breakfast sold his
birth right (his right that belonged unto
him in that he was the eldest)." Since the
Oxford English Dictionary claims Coverdale
first used this word in his 1535 Bible, it is
certain that Tyndale in fact coined the
word for his 1534 revision to avoid the
lengthy alternative.

A large de luxe copy with gilt edges, printed on vellum,
with the illustrations and initial letters of each book carefully
coloured, was presented to Anne Boleyn, now at the height
of her short-lived queenly power. A further edition quickly
followed in December, the demand was so great, and
Tyndale continued his laborious work to improve it, making
some three hundred and fifty alterations, chiefly to the style.
In 1536, just ten years after Tyndale had seen the first
English New Testament through the press at Worms, his
New Testament was actually printed in England. Times
were changing and this book had changed them. But it was
then that the blow fell.

CHAPTER 8

THE TRAITOR'S HAND
1535-1536

Henry Phillips arrived in Antwerp during the early summer of 1535. He came from a wealthy and therefore notable family in Devon and Somerset and his father, Richard, had been three times a member of parliament and twice high sheriff. Richard Phillips lived at Charborough, just five miles from Poole in Dorset, although he owned property in many places including an estate at Corfe Mullen. In addition he held the lucrative post of Controller of the Customs in Poole Harbour. Henry Phillips was the third and last son in the family and in 1533 he registered at Oxford for a degree in civil law and, being a man of some ability, was set fair to gain a good position and follow a respectable life. However, Henry Phillips had a side to his character that only now came into the open. Entrusted with a large sum of money by his father to pay to someone in London, Henry reached the big city and gambled away his charge. What his movements were immediately after that we cannot be sure, but three years later in the winter of 1536-7 he wrote from the Continent a series of long, penitent letters home expressing his terrible poverty and the fact that his dire straits would soon end his life in abject misery unless his parents held out a hand of forgiveness and assistance. He was by then being branded as a traitor and rebel, and had found himself the object of attention by government agents and without a friend in the world. Henry wrote ingratiatingly to his mother, his father, his two brothers, two brothers-in-law and others known to the family. He even sent letters to his father baked in a loaf of bread to help them reach home without falling into un-friendly hands. But these letters were apparently all inter-cepted by Cromwell's agents.

After squandering his father's money in London, Phillips had evidently come into contact with someone who was still anxious to apprehend Tyndale. Phillips was virtually stranded in the capital, afraid to return home and unable to leave the city. A young educated man from the university, with influential connections and a known hatred for the king and the reformers, and now in a terrible financial mess, was the ideal person to send upon a new mission to kidnap Tyndale. We may never know the identity of the powerful dignitary who so successfully used Phillips as his front man in the arrest of Tyndale, but a few weeks after the accomplishment of his terrible assignment, Phillips was waiting nervously in Louvain for the return of his servant from England; the servant had been sent home with an urgent despatch and Phillips was anxious lest Cromwell should intercept the successful report. Clearly the servant got through safely for otherwise the letter would be on record and we should know the identity of the high official behind the plot. Although bishops Gardiner, Longland and Stokesley were all capable of such craft, the prime suspicion must rest upon Stokesley, Bishop of London. His hatred of the reformers was venomous, and he boasted of the number of heretics he had killed. Beside Stokesley even Thomas More appeared gentle. It was Stokesley's red-bearded servant, John Tisen, whom Tyndale recognised in Antwerp early in 1533 and another of his servants visited the town the following July.

Whoever his master, Phillips received his orders, a servant, a liberal supply of money and set off for Louvain. Louvain was in the province of Brabant and the town, strongly against reform, was situated about thirty miles north-east of a small village of later historical importance called Waterloo. Phillips registered as a student at the university and, to explain his apparent wealth, spoke freely of holding two good benefices in the diocese of Exeter. From Louvain he could plan his strategy and ride along the direct road to Antwerp, less than thirty miles away.

Whereas John Tisen had kept himself aloof from the
English merchants, Henry Phillips threw himself into their
company and by his silver tongue and golden hand won the
confidence of all except Thomas Poyntz. It was not long
before Tyndale, who was frequently invited to dine with the
merchants, found himself in the same company, and Henry
Phillips had come face to face with his quarry. Unsuspecting,
the reformer felt attracted to the easy manner and eloquent
speech of the young student lawyer, and before long he
invited him to the home of the Poyntz family where he dined,
admired Tyndale's small library, warmly commended his
labours and talked easily of the affairs in England and the
need for reform. He even stayed overnight. Thomas Poyntz
held misgivings about the relative stranger, but when
Tyndale assured him of the man's Lutheran sympathies he
put his doubts aside. This was the greatest mistake Tyndale
ever made. Phillips won the friendship of Poyntz, and after
a few days the merchant took the visitor on a tour of Antwerp
and readily answered the enquiries about the alleys, buildings
and chief officers of the town. They talked about the king
and his affairs, Poyntz and his affairs, Phillips and his
affairs. It was all very amicable. What Poyntz only later
realised was that Phillips was also gently sounding him out
to see whether, for a good bribe, he would be willing to sacrifice Tyndale. For all his astute business abilities Poyntz did not,
apparently, pick up the veiled message until it was too late.

Within a few days Henry Phillips had gone. He had learnt
sufficient from his new friends to know that it would be
useless to work through the merchants or the officers of
Antwerp; a warning would almost certainly reach Tyndale
before he could be seized. He was right in this. Antwerp was
full of eyes, ears and mouths. As early as April of this year
the imperial attorney in Brussels had issued a warrant for the
arrest of the three leaders of English reform, Tyndale, Joye
and Dr Barnes. This warrant was passed to the leaders at
Bergen in case one of the wanted men should visit the great
trade fair held in that town in April. A helpful note warned
the Antwerp merchants of all these official communications.
Thus Phillips rode straight to the court of Brussels, twenty-

four miles distant and just a few miles west from Louvain. Ambassador Hackett had died in October 1534 and neither Henry of England nor Charles of the great Imperial Empire was in a hurry to see him replaced. Henry had finally substituted Anne and himself for Catherine and the pope; the Bishop of Rochester, John Fisher, and the recent Lord Chancellor, Thomas More, were already on their way to the scaffold; the pope was putting the finishing touches to his Bull to excommunicate this great "Defender of the Faith", and Charles, because of all this, was not talking to Henry. Phillips therefore arrived at the Imperial Court at a time when he could act as his own ambassador and with valuable information against one of Henry's subjects. With little delay he obtained the services of the Emperor's attorney and, with a small party of officers, set out on the road back to Antwerp.

Thomas Poyntz was sitting unusually lazily by his door when Phillips's servant arrived, enquired whether William Tyndale was at home, and assured the merchant that his master would shortly call back to see the translator. He did not call back, and three or four days later Poyntz left Antwerp to conduct his business at Barrow, some eighteen miles from the town. He expected to be away for a month or six weeks and Phillips, knowing this, decided to strike without further delay. He arrived at the home of Mrs Poyntz about May 21st, 1535, and, in his courteous and charming manner, invited himself to lunch. He then returned into the town, presumably to set the officers in their appropriate place for ambush. Phillips' plan was working admirably, only requiring that Tyndale, who had already been invited out to lunch that day, cancel the arrangement made with Mrs Poyntz and invite Phillips to join him in the town. In this he was not disappointed. But Henry Phillips could not resist one more victory over his already condemned prize. Almost as an afterthought he asked Tyndale if he would kindly lend him two pounds on the pretext that he had, that very morning, lost his purse. Tyndale, "simple and inexpert in the wily subtleties of this world", handed over the money (enough for a poor family to live on for two months) and so the two men left the house.

Tyndale's arrest

Antwerp was, like all mediaeval towns, laced with twisting, narrow alleys that in places refused to allow two men to pass and were so sunless by reason of the overhanging buildings that the pedestrians might have to bump in order to meet. As they left Poyntz's home just such an opening confronted them. Tyndale courteously stepped back to allow his guest to precede him. Phillips, a tall, handsome man, stood aside and insisted that the great reformer should have precedence. Tyndale came to the opening and saw two officers ready to seize him, he hesitated and moved back, Phillips stood over him, pointing down with his finger as a sign that this was the man; he then jostled Tyndale forward into the officers who bound him with ropes and brought him to the attorney's residence and finally to the grim castle of Vilvorde, just six miles north of Brussels.

The castle of Vilvorde had been erected in 1374 by one of the dukes of Brabant and since it was modelled upon the infamous Bastille, built in Paris at about the same time, its moat, seven towers, three drawbridges and massive walls made it an impregnable prison. The castle was used as the state prison for the Low Countries, and Tyndale was thrown into one of the foul-smelling, damp dungeons with nothing for company but the lapping moat and the squabbling moorhens outside and the dripping walls and scurrying rats inside. Here, in his solitary darkness, Tyndale waited for the end. The merchants, with all their power at Antwerp, were powerless here and few would risk their livelihood to try to save him. His work that remained undone could never be completed. Tyndale knew he had finished the course.

ATTEMPTS AT RESCUE

When Thomas Poyntz galloped into Antwerp in reply to the urgent message from his wife, he discovered Tyndale's room ransacked and all his books and papers taken. Poyntz was furious. He blamed himself, he blamed the merchants, he blamed the governor of the English House, he blamed Tyndale's simplicity but above all he blamed the authorities. This was an outrageous breach of the traditional privilege of the house of the English merchants. And the merchants lost no time in sending a strong letter of protest to the government of the Low Countries. Letters of indignant complaint poured into the court at Brussels. Letters also began to arrive at the court of Henry. And behind all this action was the never tiring hand of faithful Thomas Poyntz. But it was a forlorn hope. Charles V was making up for lost time by turning upon the Lutherans with a vengeance and Henry VIII, having toppled the pope over the cliffs of England, was anxious to prove he was still a loyal Roman Catholic and certainly no heretic. Just to demonstrate his point, fourteen Dutch anabaptists were sent to the stake in England within a few days of Tyndale's arrest. Thomas Cromwell could do very little even if he had wanted to; his own neck was scarcely more secure than that of his predecessor. He sent an agent, who checked upon Phillips and found him thirsting for the death of Tyndale, the arrest of Joye and Barnes, and the misfortune of the king; the agent talked with the merchants and clucked sympathetically. But what could be done?

Thomas Poyntz determined to do something. He wrote to his brother John, who was lord of the manor of North Ockenden in Essex, and urged him to make representation in the court. The death of Tyndale, Poyntz urged, "will be a great hindrance to the Gospel, and, to the enemies of it, one of the highest pleasures". The king never had a more loyal subject than Tyndale or a man of higher reputation. Poyntz's letter breathes a zeal and loyalty to the reformer that reveals the close relationship between the two men and their common faith in Christ. Meanwhile, Cromwell was beginning to stir; by the middle of August he consulted the king, and, receiving a favourable royal reply, wrote two letters to members of the privy council at Brabant. Since Tyndale stood unquestionably condemned by the German laws against heretics, the only hope was to request his extradition to England.

One of these letters was addressed to the Marquis of Bergen and since he had just left Brussels for Germany, Poyntz was commissioned to ride after him and bring back

a reply to Antwerp. Poyntz caught up with the lordly party
at Alken but received such a cold verbal reply that the
importunate merchant offered to follow the Marquis to the
next overnight stop in order to give his lordship time to
think over the matter. At Maestricht Poyntz received a
reasonable reply and rode straight to Brussels. From Brussels
he went to England and by the beginning of November
returned to the Imperial Court. This scurrying to and fro
almost succeeded, for the court was on the point of delivering
Tyndale to Poyntz to be taken to England, when Henry
Phillips stepped in. Terrified that he might lose his quarry,
Phillips accused Thomas Poyntz of the very charges that had
been laid against Tyndale and the poor merchant found
himself under arrest! Poyntz was interrogated, a list of
charges were drawn up and he was given time to reply in
writing. It was impossible for him to do more for his friend
in Vilvorde Castle until he was himself a free man, but
unfortunately that would take time. Poyntz knew that unless
he could escape there was no possibility of avoiding the
supreme penalty. By constant and ingenious excuses the
merchant put off his reply and by Christmas was still under
arrest. By the end of January his reply was complete. But
Poyntz was desperate to escape. He was accomplishing
nothing for Tyndale, his own business interests were being
sadly neglected. Phillips had everything going his own way
and, on top of all this, Poyntz was being charged at the rate
of five shillings a day for the privilege of having two guards
to prevent his escape. After thirteen weeks Poyntz had had
enough. One night he slipped from the house, eluded his
guards and, at the opening of the city gate, left Brussels and
fled to England. Meanwhile poor John Baers was fined eighty
pounds for having "through breach of duty and negligence"
permitted the escape of "a prisoner accused of Lutheranism,
named Thomas Poyntz, an Englishman".

Although he failed in his attempt to rescue his friend it
must stand to the credit of Poyntz that he gave himself
unstintingly to the service of Tyndale. He was banished from
the Low Countries, lost most of his merchant interests in
consequence, was separated from his wife and family for

The Castle of Vilvorde

many years and when he finally succeeded to his brother's estate at North Ockenden, he was too poor to live there. He died in 1562 and his epitaph in the church at North Ockenden speaks of his suffering and imprisonment, "for faithful service to his prince and ardent profession of evangelical truth".

It is little comfort to know that for his Judas-like betrayal Henry Phillips gained nothing either. He spent the next few years fleeing from Henry's agents. They reached him in Rome and then in Paris where he arrived "altogether ragged and torn", and where he stole some clothes from an old friend who helped him. He once returned to London but was forced back to Louvain from where he wrote those begging letters home. In the autumn of 1538 he arrived in Italy as a Swiss mercenary with German boots having walked from Flanders. By 1542 he passes from history as a prisoner under threat of losing his eyes or his life. Disowned by his family, by his country, by almost every prince on the continent and even by those with whom he collaborated in his terrible crime, he died, Foxe conjectures, "consumed at last with lice".

The bid to rescue Tyndale was virtually exhausted. Stephen Vaughan was in the Low Countries in March and still held some hope of success if only Cromwell would give him more letters, but Vaughan must have been more optimistic than realistic by now. By September Pope Julius III had finally summoned the courage to excommunicate the king for divorcing Catherine, "without any lawful cause". The Bull included "his accomplices, abettors, adherents and followers, and persons in any manner culpable in the premises". The king was given sixty days to appear before the pope in person or by proxy otherwise he would "incur the deprivation of his kingdom and aforesaid dominions". For good measure the Holy Father concluded, "We strike them with the sword of anathema malediction and eternal damnation". All England was given the choice of excommunication by the pope or excommunication by the king. And since everyone was forbidden to trade with the king, all Europe had the same choice. Admittedly the pope later withdrew the Bull and claimed he had never meant it (even though he reapplied it two years later), but 1536 was not a good year for Henry anywhere.

A BAD YEAR FOR THE KING AND THE MONASTERIES

In fact, for Henry, the year appeared to begin quite well; Catherine died in January. But even she spoilt the king's pleasure at the occasion by declaring herself in her dying hours, "Catherine, Queen of England". Ten days later Henry fell in the jousts and was unconscious for two hours. An ulcerated leg was causing him intense pain and the plague had broken out in London. To add to all his trials, Anne Boleyn had an unfortunate miscarriage of a baby boy, and the poor queen found her friends slipping aside as more and more charges were heaped against her by her merciless enemies. In May the king imported a French executioner who skilfully severed Anne's slender neck and the following day Henry moved Jane Seymour from Wiltshire into the vacated apartments of the girl from Sussex. By the month of October disquieting reports of a rebel uprising in the north reached His Majesty's ears; and all because of a Bill he had signed earlier in the year.

This was the year when Henry began his suppression of the smaller monasteries. By dissolving all the monasteries and abbeys with an income of under two hundred pounds a year, the king could add some twenty thousand pounds to his own income and prepare the way for the same treatment of the larger religious houses two years later. Cromwell sent out his commissioners to lay charges against their inmates and show the nation that suppression was the only way to reform. Superiors, monks and nuns were sent out with a state pension and the monastic property was sold and, in many cases, the buildings left for the poor villagers to use as a stone quarry. In fact history has been unduly harsh to Cromwell, for he only followed the example set by many before him. Almost all the religious houses in England and Wales had become firmly established by the end of the thirteenth century, and both Edward III and Henry V seized monastic property when it suited them; the difference was only in degree: "Henry V breakfasted and Henry VIII dined". Even Henry's father had dissolved the convent of St. Radegund at Cambridge to find sufficient money for the foundation of Jesus College.

Staunch churchmen also had set a good precedent for Cromwell. Bishop Fisher of Rochester, who years later laid his head on the block in defence of the pope, obtained papal Bulls and a king's licence to dissolve two nunneries, one at Higham near Rochester and the other at Bramhall in Salisbury. To justify his actions Fisher produced stories of lasciviousness and debauchery as lurid as anything that came from the pen of Cromwell's agents: and no-one challenged *his* accuracy. Besides, it was all in a good cause, for St. John's, Cambridge came from this. And good causes were the excuse for Cardinal Wolsey also. As soon as he became a life legate of the pope in 1518 he set out to dissolve twenty-seven monasteries to endow his new Cardinal's College at Oxford (now Christ Church) and his Grammar School at Ipswich; and some of these monasteries were quite large. In fact Thomas Cromwell served his apprenticeship under Wolsey in this round of suppressions from 1524 to 1529. It all came under the heading of reform. The Benedictines squealed loudly. "If the reformation is conducted with too much authority," they urged, "there will not be enough monks to inhabit the monasteries. At the present time, now the world is drawing to its end, very few desire to live an austere life."

The Benedictines' eschatology may have left much to be desired, but they were right about the changing times. This is precisely what Cromwell found in 1536. In addition to the dissolute life of many of the monks and nuns, and as we have seen, Morton, Fisher, Wolsey, Colet, More and Erasmus knew all about this even if some modern historians do not, Cromwell found something more. He found hundreds of monks and nuns glad to leave their religious prison houses. In Sussex, of the seven houses reported on, only four of the forty-two monks wished to remain in their orders. Letters came regularly into Cromwell's hands, from monks who had been forced into their religious orders at the age of thirteen, and younger, and who longed to be released. And the reason was often startling. Many had been affected by the new teaching and by the books of Tyndale and Luther. The Prior of the Abbey at Reading had bought sixty forbidden books and was transferred to the Tower for his pains. A monk at Evesham wrote boldly to Cromwell, "I study Greek, Latin and Hebrew and refute papistical sophistry". Bishop Nix of Norwich complained bitterly of the effect Tyndale's New Testament and books were having. Speaking of the suppression of Gonville Hall in 1530, he had declared there was "no monk who had lately come out of it but smelleth of the frying pan". Bishop Nix clearly had a simple remedy for heretics! Even the monks in the great Abbey of Hayles in Tyndale's own county of Gloucester were affected by his teaching; at Kingswood in the same county the prior was writing in favour of the King's Supremacy, and that not merely to save his neck. And so the story could continue. It was the New Testament that was causing reform, nothing else. Kings and Cardinals could only suppress monasteries, the Word of God could reform men.

But of course it was not all like this. The bitter opposition in the north to the king's action brought Henry, in October 1536, to the most dangerous month of his reign. However, with the aid of the duke of Norfolk, a few gracious words, a mound of broken promises and a liberal use of the block and gallows, the king arrived safely, if just a little shaken, at the close of the year.

THE DUNGEON OF VILVORDE

Meanwhile Tyndale, shivering in the dungeons of the Castle of Vilvorde, was too great a man to entertain any petty hopes for revenge over Henry Phillips. He had never expected his death to be other than violent; he had been too long exposed to the dangerous life of the hunted exile to waste time mourning his present state. His trial would be little more than a formality, but in the event he might have opportunity for speaking of his Saviour and thus he must prepare his defence well. In addition, he continued with the work so close to his heart, and what time and light were available to him Tyndale used to press on with his writing and translation.

Tyndale at work in his prison cell

The queen-regent appointed the commission that was to try Tyndale. The names of the commissioners, and even how much they were paid for the job, have all found their way down the avenues of history. The attorney was of course included, for Tyndale was a very important prisoner, three theologians from Louvain followed, and the inquisitor of the Low Countries, four members of council, all lawyers presumably, and nine servants and messengers completed the commission. The attorney received one hundred and twenty-eight pounds and the three theologians and the inquisitor shared one hundred and forty-nine pounds. Out of the meagre property of the reformer, confiscated from his room at Antwerp, the cost of his food and guards was deducted at the rate, like Poyntz, of five shillings a day. According to the accounts, Tyndale was imprisoned for one year and one hundred and thirty-five days and the lieutenant of the castle was paid one hundred and two pounds. Presumably Tyndale's money ran out before his execution. The whole cost of his trial and execution amounted to four hundred and seven pounds, nine shillings and sixpence.

When Tyndale stood before the commission he faced the thin, close-pressed lips, hard eyes and cold and forbidding face of James Masson, one of the theologians from Louvain. Masson possessed a brilliant mind but an icy heart and small body and he was equally opposed to Erasmus as he was to Luther. Ruard Tapper was chancellor of the university of Louvain and from his later life as inquisitor of the Low Countries we learn of his utter ruthlessness in dealing with all heretics. Even his supporters agreed that his policy was one of iron extermination of all things new and that to sacrifice a few important victims, whether they were guilty or not, served to terrify the common people into submission. His narrow, intolerant face and piercing eyes promised little mercy for Tyndale. The attorney was well known as a man of heartless, cold-blooded cruelty who would not hesitate to interrupt proceedings to send a prisoner for torture in order to extract fresh evidence.

The doctors came and went from Tyndale's cell questioning, prying, threatening; and ever at hand was Henry Phillips just in case he could be of assistance. Phillips hovered about the cell door, half afraid of meeting the eyes of the humble, godly reformer. Tyndale was seized in May and three months passed before a sample of his work was translated into Latin ready for the trial. In all probability the prosecution was not ready before the beginning of the new year of 1536. The defendant was offered an advocate, but he preferred to conduct his own defence; the Gospel he had so laboured to uphold he would defend himself. He had not been idle. The preliminaries to such trials consisted of a war of paper, each side producing arguments and counter arguments. The prosecution of course, could never lose, but the chief object was to gain as much evidence as possible from the prisoner's own hand so that a few choice quotations would easily secure a sentence.

Tyndale toiled away. As the autumn of 1535 faded, his chest and head laboured with heavy catarrh; he shivered through the day and shivered all night as well. As he penned his little treatise *Faith alone Justifies before God,* winter drew on and the light began to fail; a few hours a day was all he could use for writing. The remainder of the time he sat in darkness. But he must finish his work for this was to be his summary of the evangelical Gospel; since he was going to die anyway, there must be no doubt as to *why* he died. The great doctors sat in their warm libraries with servants scurrying for books and more logs for the fire, defending the false doctrines of the popes against the small reformer, coughing and shivering over his defence of the truth in the dungeons of Vilvorde Castle.

Tyndale pushed aside his defence and drew a fresh sheet of paper in front of him. The winter of 1535 was harsh and though he was too bold for Christ to plead for release, and too wise to consider it of any value if he had, he determined to request the prison governor, who happened to be the Marquis of Bergen, for a few essentials to help him with his study, and to maintain a little longer the flickering life that shivered in his body. The letter was written in Latin and it is the only letter in Tyndale's own hand that has survived:

"I believe, right worshipful, that you are not unaware

of what may have been determined concerning me. Wherefore I beg your lordship, and that by the Lord Jesus, that if I am to remain here through the winter, you will request the commissary to have the kindness to send me, from the goods of mine which he has, a warmer cap; for I suffer greatly from cold in the head, and am afflicted by a perpetual catarrh, which is much increased in this cell; a warmer coat also, for this which I have is very thin; a piece of cloth too to patch my leggings. My overcoat is worn out; my shirts are also worn out. He has a woollen shirt, if he will be good enough to send it. I have also with him leggings of thicker cloth to put on above; he has also warmer night caps. And I ask to be allowed to have a lamp in the evening; it is indeed wearisome sitting alone in the dark. But most of all I beg and beseech your clemency to be urgent with the commissary, that he will kindly permit me to have the Hebrew Bible, Hebrew grammar, and Hebrew dictionary, that I may pass the time in that study. In return may you obtain what you most desire, so only that it be for the salvation of your soul. But if any other decision has been taken concerning me, to be carried out before winter, I will be patient, abiding the will of God, to the glory of the grace of my Lord Jesus Christ; whose Spirit (I pray) may ever direct your heart.   Amen.

W. Tindalus."

This letter is typical of Tyndale; there is no cringing flattery, no frantic plea for mercy, no long and tedious defence or protests of loyalty, faithful service, humble obedience and so on, all of which is so familiar in letters from sixteenth century condemned cells. Tyndale asks for his needs, determines to go on with his study, longs only for the salvation of his captors and is ready for whatever God's sovereign purpose may be. Whether his request was granted cannot yet be told.

But Tyndale was not altogether alone. The stream of visitors was at times endless. It was quite common for such a prisoner to be allowed virtually unlimited visits. But few of these, if any, would be from friends of the Gospel. The fate of poor Thomas Poyntz was sufficient to deter them. Visitors

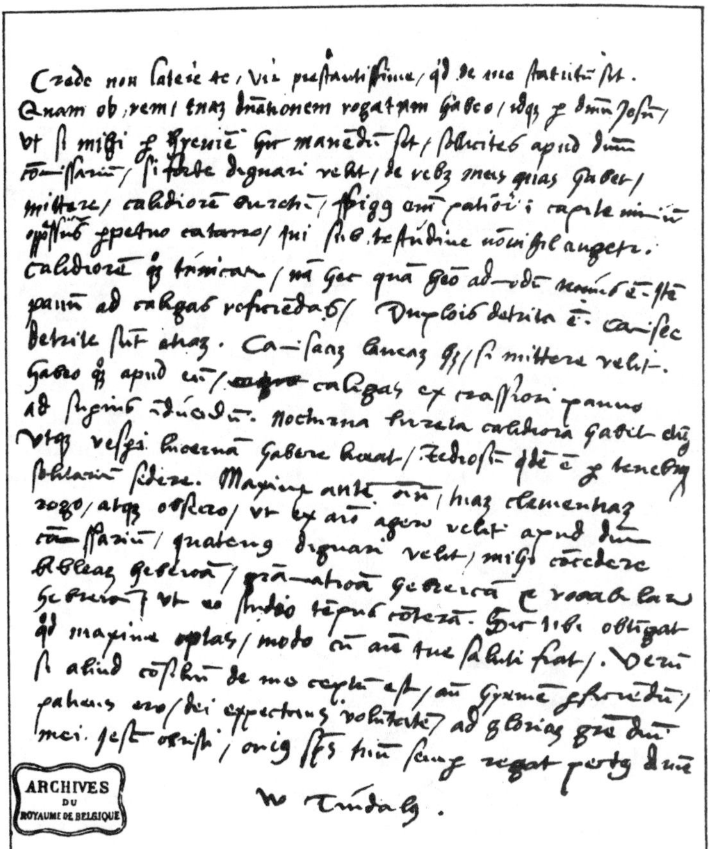
Credo non latere te, vir praestantissime, quid de me statutum sit.
Quam ob rem, tuam dominationem rogatum habeo, idque per dominum Jesum,
ut si mihi per hiemem hic manendum sit, solicites apud dominum
commissarium, si forte dignari velit, de rebus meis quas habet,
mittere, calidiorem birretum, frigus enim patior in capite nimium,
perpetuo catarro, qui sub testudine nonnihil augetur.
Calidiorem quoque tunicam, nam haec quam habeo admodum tenuis est. Item
pannum ad caligas reficiendas. Duplois detrita est. Camiseae
detritae sunt etiam. Camiseam laneam habet, si mittere velit.
Habeo quoque apud eum, caligas ex crassiori panno
ad superinduendum. Nocturna birreta calidiora habet etiam.
Vespere lucernam habere liceat, taediosum quidem est per tenebras
solitarium sedere. Maxime autem omnium tuam clementiam
rogo atque obsecro, ut ex animo agere velit apud dominum
commissarium, quatenus dignari velit mihi concedere
Bibliam Hebraicam, grammaticam Hebraicam et vocabularium
Hebraicum, ut eo studio tempus conteram. Sic tibi obtingat
quod maxime optas, modo cum animae tuae salute fiat. Verum
si aliud consilium de me ceptum est, ante hiemem perficiendum,
patiens ero, Dei expectans voluntatem, ad gloriam gratiae domini
mei Jesu Christi, cujus spiritus tuum semper regat pectus. Amen.
W. Tindalus.

Tyndale's last letter

would come into Tyndale's cell to argue, debate and try to gain renown by persuading the arch-heretic to recant. But the sturdy convictions and gracious life of Tyndale influenced many in the castle. Foxe tells us that his keeper, the keeper's daughter and others of his household were converted by this witness, and that others in the castle confirmed that if Tyndale was not a true Christian, then there was no such thing.

This great reformer, cold and cramped in the dungeons of Vilvorde, could not be aware of another great man preparing to take up the truths of Reformation doctrine. John Calvin, a brilliant academic who had been converted only four years, was sitting at his desk nearly three-hundred miles away in the town of Basel in Switzerland, bordering France, and Germany. Calvin, in hiding and writing under an assumed name, was preparing for the press a small treatise entitled *Institutes of the Christian Religion*. This little book, published in the Spring of 1536, would swell over the next quarter of a century into the "bulky but compact and thoroughly organized textbook of theology"[1] that was possibly the most outstanding and influential production of sixteenth century Reformation literature. As one Gospel torch was extinguished, God saw to it that another was, at that very moment, being lit.

THE BURNING TRIAL

The long awaited trial began. Tyndale had been in the castle for eighteen months and now everything was set. A long list of charges was drawn up.

"*First*, he had maintained that faith alone justifies.

Second, he maintained that to believe in the forgiveness of sins and to embrace the mercy offered in the Gospel, was enough for salvation.

Third, he averred that human traditions cannot bind the conscience, except where their neglect might occasion scandal.

Fourth, he denied the freedom of the will.

---

[1] Quotation from B. B. Warfield, *Calvin and Augustine*.

Fifth, he denied that there is any purgatory.

Sixth, he affirmed that neither the Virgin nor the Saints pray for us in their own person.

Seventh, he asserted that neither the Virgin nor the Saints should be invoked by us."

And so the list continued. There was nothing new, either in the charges or the long reams of paper that had gone back and forth between the castle dungeons and the doctors at Louvain. Tyndale had said it all before.

Early in August 1536 the reformer was condemned as a heretic. A few days later the pageant of casting him out of the Church took place. In the town square a crowd gathered and the great doctors and dignitaries assembled in due pomp and array, and took their seats on the high platform. Tyndale was led out, wearing his priest's robes. He was made to kneel and his hands were scraped with a knife or a piece of glass as a symbol of having lost the benefits of the anointing oil with which he was consecrated to the priesthood. The bread and wine of the mass were placed in his hands and at once withdrawn. This done, he was ceremoniously stripped of his priest's vestments, reclothed as a lay man and handed over to the attorney for secular punishment. The Church would condemn, but always left it to the secular officers to stain their hands with the murder. But for Tyndale the end was not yet. He was taken back to Vilvorde Castle and for some unexplained reason remained a prisoner for two more months. Doubtless priests and monks visited him in their droves, all eager to write their names in the register of Roman favour by being the man who forced Tyndale to recant. But this man was a rock and the tired prisoner met his attackers with a calm serenity. As well move the castle itself by a drizzle of rain as persuade William Tyndale to recant. His mind and faith were fixed and He whom Tyndale had served so faithfully would not leave His servant alone in his hour of need.

One day, early in the month of October 1536, William Tyndale was led out of the castle towards the southern gate of the town. The sun had barely risen above the horizon when he arrived at the open space and looked over the crowd

eagerly jostling for a good view. A circle of stakes enclosed
the place of execution and in the centre was a large pillar of
wood in the form of a cross and as tall as a man. A strong
chain hung from the top and a noose of hemp was threaded
through a hole in the upright. The attorney and the great
doctors arrived first and seated themselves in state nearby.
The prisoner was brought in and a final appeal was made
that he should recant. Would he yet deny the faith for which
so many of his friends had died? Could he renounce the words
he had solemnly declared over the years? Tyndale stood
immovable, his keen eyes gazed towards the common people
whom he pitied for their ignorance; he met the cruel and
merciless stare of his judges and doubtless pitied them also. A
silence fell over the crowd as they watched the lean form and
thin, tired face of the prisoner; his lips moved with a final
impassionate prayer that echoed round the stillness of that
place of execution and reached to the God who controls the
counsels of men: "Lord, open the King of England's eyes".

Tyndale moved towards the cross. His feet were bound to
the stake, the iron chain fastened around his neck, and the
hemp noose was placed at his throat. Only the anabaptists
and lapsed heretics were burnt alive. Tyndale was spared
that ordeal. Piles of brushwood and logs were heaped
around him. The executioner came up behind the stake and
with all his force snapped down upon the noose. Within
seconds Tyndale was strangled. The attorney stepped
forward, placed a lighted torch to the tinder and the great
men and commoners sat back to watch the fire burn. Not
until the charred form hung limply on the chain did an officer
break out the staple of the chain with his halbert, allowing
the body to fall into the glowing heat of the fire; more
brushwood was piled on top and, whilst the commoners
marvelled "at the patient sufference of Master Tyndale at
the time of his execution", the attorney and the doctors of
Louvain moved off to begin their day's work.

*   *   *

In the year of Tyndale's death two Bibles were circulating
in England; one came from the pen of Miles Coverdale and

the other, called Matthew's Bible, came from the pen of
John Rogers, the converted chaplain of the English House in
Antwerp. Both Bibles were dedicated to his Majesty and
waited his Royal consent. Both contained Tyndale's New
Testament virtually unaltered, and were heavily dependent
upon his Pentateuch and parts of the rest of the Old Testament. The king ran his eyes over Coverdale's Bible. Tyndale's
name did not appear, and the bishops assured him they could
find no errors. "Then if there be no heresies" roared Henry,
"in God's name, let it go abroad among the people". The
following year his Majesty authorised a small phrase of
immense significance to be added to the foot of the title page
of Matthew's Bible: "Set forth with the kinges most gracyous
lycense". On September 5th, 1538 Henry ordered every
church in England to display "one book of the whole
Bible of the largest volume in English", the cost to be
borne equally by the parson and the parishioners. Among
other injunctions the people were urged to learn the Lord's
Prayer, the Creed and the Ten Commandments in English,
the very crime for which those seven poor folk were burnt
at Coventry in 1519. Even in the year of Tyndale's death
Bishop Fox of Hereford declared in convocation, "The lay
people do now know the Holy Scripture better than many of
us". By 1539 the king had received so many complaints that
the people gathering around the chained Bible were reading
it so loudly, even during the celebration of mass, that His
Majesty ordered them to refrain from reading the Bible
during divine services. On November 14th, 1539 the king sent
to all "printers and sellers of books" a royal encouragement
for the "free and liberal use of the Bible in our own maternal
English tongue". As if to anticipate the king, Robert Redman
was printing Tyndale's translation in 1538, and his printshop
was next door to St. Dunstan's where the great reformer once
preached.

The Lord had answered the dying prayer of Tyndale. All
England had its Bible. Tyndale was the heart of the Reformation in England because he weaned it from negative
opposition and gave it spiritual life, but he was also its head
because he stopped it beating Rome with the mere words of

men and gave it the Word of God. Others, both inside and outside the Church of Rome, had shown the abuses, but no-one before or after him showed so plainly the cause of these abuses and how they could be healed. For Tyndale it was not enough to cry *Sola Scriptura*, Scripture alone, men must have that Scripture to read. By the untainted quality of his life and unstinted devotion of his scholarship William Tyndale first gave to England what the nation has never yet lost, the English New Testament in print. The work of Tyndale that first issued from the printshop at Worms and was smuggled into England just four hundred and fifty years ago, is now read by millions throughout the English speaking world. But, typical of the man who hid himself away that his Lord might be exalted, his work comes within the covers of the Authorised Version of King James. Others, like Coverdale and Rogers, might receive the acclaim but the achievement belongs solely to Tyndale. He stood almost alone among Englishmen when the king, the bishops and all Europe threw their weight against him. Within a few years of his death, the king, the bishops and all Europe were beginning to awaken to the need of the Scriptures in English. It was not that Tyndale's translation, under the cloak of Coverdale and Rogers, was accepted because times were changing. On the contrary, it was Tyndale's translation that was changing the times and thus the whole course of English history. William Tyndale *was* the Reformation in England.

We can honour Tyndale's memory in no greater way than by taking those same Scriptures as our only guide into the truth of God's way of Salvation, and *that* will honour Tyndale's God.

BIBLIOGRAPHY

BIBLIOGRAPHY

GENERAL

The Reformation in England	Merle d'Aubigné	Banner of Truth 1963
Tudor Puritanism	M. M. Knappen	University of Chicago Press 1939
The Annals of the English Bible	Christopher Anderson	Jackson, Watford and Hodder. 1862.
Letters to Cromwell and Others on the Suppression of the Monasteries	G. H. Cook	John Baker. 1965
English Monks and the Suppression of the Monasteries	G. Baskerville	Jonathan Cape. 1937
Religion at Oxford and Cambridge	V. H. H. Green	S.C.M. Press Ltd. 1964
The History of the Popes (Vol. v-x)	Dr Ludwig Pastor	Keegan Paul, Trench, Trubner and Co. Ltd. 1898
England's Earliest Protestants	W. A. Glebsch	Yale University Press 1964
Army Royal	C. G. Cruickshank	Oxford, Clarendon 1969
Life on the English Manor	H. S. Bennett	Cambridge. 1965

An Age of Ambition	F. R. H. DuBoulay	Nelson. 1970
Life in Mediaeval England	J. J. Bagley	B. T. Batsford Ltd. 1960
Pennant's London	Thomas Pennant	Faulder and Crosby. 1813
Mediaeval London	Benham and Welch	Seeley and Co. Ltd. 1901
History of the English Bible	B. F. Westcott	Macmillan and Co. 1872
The Acts and Monuments of the Church	John Fox	
Europe in the Sixteenth Century	A. H. Johnson	Rivingtons. 1903
A History of the Reformation in the Low Countries	Gerrard Brandt	London. 1719
Books: From Papyrus to Paperbacks	Harley and Hampden	Methuen. 1964
Five Hundred Years of Printing	Steinberg	Pellican. 1955 and 1974

BOOKS AND PAPERS FROM GLOUCESTER LIBRARY

Tyndale's Knowledge of Hebrew	Extract from the Journal of Theological Studies—Oct. 1935 Vol. 36. No. 144. J. F. Mozley	
The Tyndales in Gloucestershire	J. H. Cooke	C. T. Jefferies and Sons. 1877
Good and Great Men of Gloucestershire	Joseph Stratford	C. H. Savary. 1867
History of Gloucestershire	Thos. Rudge	G. F. Harris. 1803
The Editions of the New Testament—Tyndale's Versions 1525-1566	Francis Fry	Henry Sotheran. 1878
Erasmus, Tyndale and More	W. E. Campbell	Eyre and Spottiswoode 1949
Sixteenth Century Bristol	John Latimer	J. W. Arrowsmith. 1908

Transactions of the Bristol and Gloucester Archaeological Society 1882-1883. Vol. VII.

The Retrospective Review and Historical and Antiquarian
   Magazine 1829—Bristol in the Fifteenth Century.
The History of Bristol—civil and ecclesiastical—John Corry 1816.
Note: This list by no means exhausts the fine collection of
   material held by the Gloucester Public Library.

BIOGRAPHY

Henry VIII	John Bowle	Allen and Unwin. 1964
Henry VIII	J. J. Bagley	B. T. Batsford Ltd. 1962
Henry VIII	C. H. Collette	W. H. Allen. 1864
Thomas More	R. W. Chambers	Jonathan Cape. 1935
More's Utopia	Everyman's Library	J. M. Dent and Sons Ltd. 1951
More's Confutation of Tyndale		Yale University Press. 1973
Naked to Mine Enemies (Cardinal Wolsey)	Charles Ferguson	Longmans, Green and Co. 1958
Life of Dean Colet	J. H. Lupton	George Bull and Sons. 1887
Life and Letters of Erasmus	J. A. Froude	Longmans, Green and Co. 1895.
Luther and His Times	E. G. Schwiebert	Concordia Publishing House. 1950
Luther	Richard Friedenthal	Weidenfeld and Nicolson. 1967
Homes and Haunts of Luther	John Stoughton	Religious Tract Soc. 1883
Life of Cranmer	C. H. Collette	George Redway. 1887
The Life of Dr Barnes	(Works of Thos. More)	Yale University Press. 1973

TYNDALE

William Tyndale	R. Demaus	Religious Tract Society. 1886
William Tyndale	G. Barnett Smith	S. W. Partridge and Co. c. 1900
William Tyndale	J. F. Mozley	S.P.C.K. 1937
William Tyndale	C. H. Williams	Thos. Nelson and Co. Ltd. 1969
The Work of William Tyndale	ed. G. E. Duffield	Fortress Press, Philadelphia. 1965
The Work of William Tyndale	ed. S. L. Greenslade	Blackie and Son Ltd. 1938
The Obedience of A Christian Man	William Tyndale	R.T.S. orig. 1528 (Christian Classics Series)
The New Testament of Tyndale 1526		Bagster. 1836
The New Testament of Tyndale 1534		Cambridge University Press. 1938

GENERAL INDEX

GENERAL INDEX

SCRIPTURE INDEX

Other books by the same author published by Evangelical Press:

Through Many Dangers
The story of John Newton

Nothing but the Truth
An explanation of the inspiration and authority of the Bible

Not by Chance
Making sense out of suffering

Shall we Dance?
Dance and drama in worship